Could We
CHANGE
—the—
WORLD?

NORAH LANG

Ordering Information:
For orders and inquiries, please contact:
books@authorsnote360.com
www.authorsnote360.com

Printed in the United States of America

CONTENTS

INTRODUCTION

O ur world constantly changes, but not always as fast as or in the ways we desire. In reality, rather than change the world around us, what we can do is change our behavior and our thinking and our relation to the world around us. I hope my efforts to apply the cognitive behavioral method in my practice of counseling clients will be useful and practical to a broad range of both professional and unenlightened readers who are interested in improving their mental health and changing their lives in the best way.

The attractiveness of this method consists in its simplicity, accessibility, and proximity to the desirable results, and also its potential to preserve and restore mental health and make our existence better. We need a change in our internal worlds and our surrounding environments because we deserve better lives and because we set this goal in the society, which was built by imaginations of our ancestors. My conclusions are not the results of scientific study; rather, they are the results of my own observations and analysis of the works of other theorists and practitioners. My motive and inspiration to compare known literature and data with my own experiences was to offer my own views while accounting for existing methods in the practice of the psychotherapy.

CHAPTER I

HOW DID THIS BEGIN?

In ancient times, the great Socrates developed his famous dialogue with a range of positive questions, each with a different focus, and created a useful test of systematic thinking that is now part of the cognitive behavioral method.

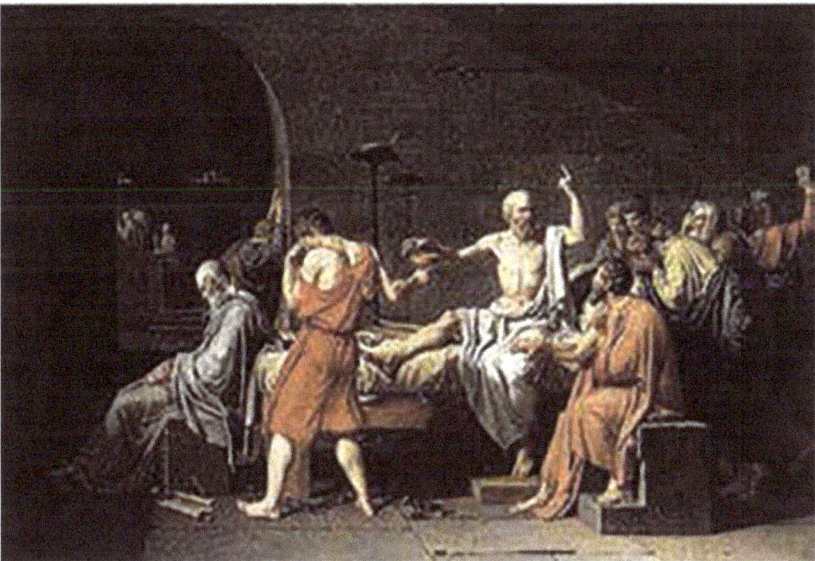

Cognitive therapy was developed by Aaron T. Beck, and it includes a short-term, present-oriented psychotherapy for patients with depression. It was designed to solve current problems and modify dysfunctional thinking and behavior (Beck 1964).

Since then, this method has also been incorporated into different areas of psychiatry. Its modification is described in detail in a book written by Paul Stallard (2005). The cognitive behavioral method in this book is particularly helpful in treating children and young people. This method has also been described in other books by various authors.

The cognitive behavioral method is designed to modify our thinking, which is connected to our feelings and behavior. Our feelings and behavior reflect our thoughts. How effortless is this? The cognitive behavioral method is based on the idea that our feelings and behavior are controlled by our thoughts. If we think negatively, we feel sad and act differently, inappropriately. If we think optimistically and positively, we feel considerably better and act correctly. So what will we select?

There is another simple explanation: our thoughts, feelings, and actions reflect the balance of the neurohormones in our brains. Thus, the cognitive behavioral method is intended to change our thoughts and behavior to enable us to feel happy, to improve our moods, and to help us achieve our goals in life by balancing the chemicals in our bodies. The very first step in the practice of this method is to gain trust and confidence in the method. The second, and no less important, step is to have patience. Results usually appear after continual practice over an extended period of time; however, in some cases they can appear quickly. This depends on how clear the patient's understanding of incorrect ways of thinking and behavior is, the level of confidence he or she has in the method, the skills of his or her therapist, how desperately the patient wants to recover, and the patient's ability to control his or her own thought processes.

How quickly results appear also depends on the ability of the therapist and the patient to formulate the positive and accurate, or the negative and inaccurate, thinking that the patient could acquire through constant practice and analysis. Thus, in my practice, the Socratic method has become irreplaceable and very useful in determining the forms and types of thinking.

The Socratic method consists of asking positive questions and then analyzing the most effective and useful explanations by establishing correct or challenging incorrect installations in the patient's thinking. This is the long way, requiring joint collaboration of the psychologist and the patient, and also great patience from both. The results of this practice can be promising, and furthermore, there are no side effects. Evidence of improvements, fewer manifestations of symptoms, prolonged improvement, and even recovery may begin. If we apply effort and utilize this method without risk, it is possible to be convinced of the truthfulness of the outline above.

I can say from experience that the Socratic method does not require complex questions that bear the positive, supporting, optimistic nature that increases patients' internal contentment with themselves. Instead, confidence of the patient is gained through sincere interest in his or her problems and personality, and based on the level of interest and erudition of the psychologist in different spheres, which is unnoticeably and not obtrusively manifested in conversations with the patient. Therefore, psychologists need to study this method in order to develop correct thinking and understanding of their own errors in thinking, which also is possible. As result, the psychologists increase their control over their own thoughts, feelings, and behaviors, and thus become examples for their patients and masters of this method.

But where should one begin? First, it is necessary to identify positive and negative self-talk. Then, based on the recollections of our childhoods (this does not include cases that involve child abuse), we must attempt to recall the tender and affectionate words we heard from our mothers, fathers, friends, different people, and other sources. Then we can try to constantly hear these words in our own mind, as our own self-talk. For example, we could hear them every morning as we are brushing our teeth. This is a good practice in difficult moments and stressful situations. Gradually our respect for ourselves and our self-confidence will grow. We learn to respect our inner-self, and we talk to our inner child and teach this inner child a new vision of the self as a good, perfect person, no matter what.

If we turn ourselves mentally to the recollections of our inner child—who never ceases to exist as a clean and innocent being, who still has sufficient time ahead of him—or herself, who hasn't made many errors, who hasn't had problems, and who deserves many credits—we can feel much better. It can be very helpful in the beginning.

If this is insufficient, we can write down positive affirmations and proposals about ourselves on a piece of paper and read them several times a day, or we can audio record them and listen to them each day. It is not worthless to think about achievements and successes instead of holding onto memories of loss. Rather, one should think about losses as a new way to success, as a new start, and as additional experience and knowledge. Sometimes the losses push us to head in a new and positive direction that might be victorious and promising. It is a fact that creating or desiring something from the positive side of our minds is more pleasant than from the dark side of our mind. In a good mood, we complete all tasks with higher energy, enthusiasm, and pleasure, which leads to the immense success.

While our negative self-talk is a great motivator, it also increases fatigue, causes depression, reduces interest, and lessens confidence in success. The fear and worries temporarily increase our ability to solve problems, and they help mobilize our attention for some time. But at the same time, we expend our energy and strength faster, lose focus, and make errors. And finally, we fail. Or if we don't fail, we experience depression, exhaustion, and fatigue. We lose interest, which leads to avoidance of people and situations that give us negative emotions. The consequence is that these neglected problems increase. Moreover, they become less solvable—or even insolvable.

When patients complain by expressing their negative thoughts, their states might be deteriorated and their symptoms exacerbated because of their concentration on negative thinking. Their trust in the cognitive behavioral method might be compromised, and the patients could end treatment. This is necessary to keep in mind. As soon as we start to identify our expression of negative self-talk, only then can real treatment begin.

As illustrated in the following scientific sources, negative thoughts can take many forms:

- *Jacqueline B. Persons (1989)*—labeling; all-or-nothing (white-and-black); the stretch-or-shrink (the magnification and minimization; exaggeration; the diminishing or disqualifying of positive); the refusing from positivism; the overgeneralization; the catastrophization; should-or-ought; the mind reader; the selective negative focus; the blaming; predicting the future; the emotional reasoning; the jumping to conclusions; the personalization
- *Robert Handly and Pauline Neff (1985)*—the perfectionism; the fear of the rejection; the negative focus; the creation of fictional fantasies; the mistaken identity
- *Paul Gilbert (1997)*—the egocentric thinking; the expecting of the punishment; self-criticism; selfattack; self-hatred; social comparison; empty of self; the expecting of the approval (the nuisance); thinking of shame; the humiliation; the revenge; the guilt; the anger; fakery; the projection
- *Keith Hawton, Paul M. Salkovskis, Joan Kirk, and David M. Clark (1989–1998)*—the confusing a thought with a fact; the assuming that only one view of things is only possible and condemning of self and others on the basis of a single event; the concentrating on weakness and forgetting of strength; the taking of responsibility in an excessive way; the double standard; the expecting and predicting only bad things; believing nothing can change in a good way

Still other types of negative thinking can be added to the list. The ability to think positive or negative thoughts is characteristic of all people, to one degree or another, and those thoughts in the normal state are in perfect balance. In some situations, the balance is disrupted but rapidly restored. If the duration and severity of the imbalance of the negative and positive thoughts are increased, then mental disease develops.

By decreasing or removing negative thinking through gaining self-control, we are freed from poor emotions, which are prevented when we feel comfortable with who we are. Feeling comfortable with who we are helps us act more adequately, reach desirable goals, and promote success in our lives. Gaining control over negative thinking gives us power over our emotions, behaviors, and future. If patients learn to control their thoughts, feelings, and behaviors, then they can improve their conditions and functioning.

Mental illness doesn't mean that all functions of the brain are disrupted or wrong. There are intermediate but normal deviations in the mental function of healthy people's brains that are reflected within normal limits in thinking and behavior. Some of these groups of people don't show their dysfunctions because they have learned to cope with them. Some people seem strange and unusual even though they are normal because they can't show adaptive enough behavior in certain situations. All of this is reflected in the classification of mental conditions and diseases adopted by American psychiatrists in the *DSM-IV* and *DSM-V*. Thus, it is necessary to keep in mind the value of negative thinking for certain groups of mentally ill and a contingent of healthy people.

Patients' awareness of their needs, for the modification of the negative thinking, depends on the intellectual levels of their development and education, their self-education, their self-consciousness, and their family structures and traditions. Expressions of feelings help identify the negative thoughts. Some people can't express their feelings because they don't have experience expressing them or don't have a suitable role model for imitation in order to gain those experiences. Others suffer this insufficiency because of genetic deviations, diseases of the prenatal and postpartum periods, the intoxications, and some medical conditions.

We all learn to express our feelings differently; for some it comes naturally, without effort. Some of us can acquire it, and some alter the expression of our feelings according to family and community requirements and general rules. We can also learn from other sources: cinema, theater, books, television, etc. Moreover, it is an interesting fact that everyone learns to repress the expression of different feelings according to life situations and play different roles as required to be acceptable in society and fit in it. However, we have a small defeating obstacle: our body language tells other people if we are bad actors.

So, communication can be a problem for both patients and healthy people too. Our thought dysfunctions show our real personalities through our body language, even when we don't want them to. Actors have learned or acquired the natural ability to control their expression of emotions and their body language harmoniously. Some people with good social skills have too. It might have been developed as some kind of protection of our internal "I" from judgment of other people in society. One author said that everybody has stupid, awkward, foolish, and nonsense thoughts; the difference is that smart people don't say them out loud.

Scientists assume that our physical and mental development determines what we look like, and how we think as a result of the selections. Some social and psychological features are determined by DNA. Unfortunately, we can't delete our unwanted DNA codes. Freud and other psychoanalysts help us understand and reveal subconscious thought. They found that our subconsciousness is predetermined by DNA, and they have obtained certain prominent results.

The cognitive behavioral method helps identify and repress the undesirable psychological features of coded DNA, or smooth their manifestations. It also helps develop new features of thinking and behavior. How are our feelings related to our ways of thinking? This is not as complicated to understand as it seems: positive thoughts are accompanied by positive emotions, and negative thoughts produce negative emotions.

How can we control our thoughts and emotions? First, we should identify negative thinking and the related emotions and how they are normal or abnormal. Second, we need to choose a new way of thinking and see if this produces an appropriate or normal emotional response. If we still haven't obtained the expected emotional response, we must reexamine how our thinking is adequate for and complies to our feelings. For this purpose, it is necessary to identify our belief systems.

Belief systems come from our childhoods, our education in our families and society, and they develop as a result of constant changes and comparisons between new accumulated experiences, observance of conventional standards in society, the requirements of a constantly changing society, and the tendency reflecting each person's DNA code. In my practice, I have observed some interesting details. Each personality follows to a different degree a system of values (beliefs) inherited from religion as common sense of life. It seems everybody, religious or not, follows the basic rules that somehow reflect the Ten Commandments.

The systems of legislation in different countries reflect those beliefs and are designed to protect those belief systems. We can subject this fact to doubt about how it happened. But regardless of the form of religion, these beliefs are the basis of religious and nonreligious societies, and all people, in essence, adhere to these principles. This makes us human, unites us, and allows us to peacefully coexist in close relation with each other. This helps us build a beautiful world together.

These values are described in different fictional books reflecting heroes who have lived on the basis of these canons. Almost all works of arts, literature, cinema, television, and newspapers contain different aspects and varieties of expression of these values. Changes in interpretation and perception of these values do not alter their essence in the human soul.

In the case of mental illness, which basically does not alter the main values of a person, we need to challenge the interpretation of basic beliefs, make corrections, and form more adaptive conclusions while implementing those corrections. The exceptions are full insanity and untreated severe mental illness, which require isolation from society and correction of the most basic values. Therefore, incorrect interpretations of systems of values (beliefs) create many types of negative and dysfunctional thinking and, as a result, cause behavioral changes that require professional assistance.

Before the epoch of psychotherapy, religious communities always existed, and they helped relieve humans' souls, clear their minds, lighten humans' sincere state, and promote enlightenment of reason.

They still serve these purposes. Science doesn't take this from religion. Rather, science improves, deepens, and clarifies confusions in interpretations. The only question is are there principles and beliefs other than basic ones? Of course. It reflects temporary beliefs created by society—fictional, imaginable, and distorted as a result of illness or lack of knowledge. But these beliefs are not reflected in the real facts. They are confused with desires that are created by manipulation, mistakes, and others reasons. All of these temporary beliefs were rejected, revised, observed, and replaced by truth—or by new confusions and manipulations.

But even if we have a clear view of all our ideals, and we choose to follow them according to our basic values and concepts, we will still encounter problems. The interpretations of our ideals can be both logical and realistic but not suitable and functional in different situations, times, and societies. Our belief systems need constant revision and correction, with the exception of basic values.

Some authors suggest that our systems of belief have to be revised, just like when we examine our wardrobes to replace certain pieces with clothing that is more modern and practical. Does the general principle in the selection of best features for our survival follow Darwin's theory? Or does it follow the intelligent design theory, which is based on the absence of evolution and believes instead that the development of life forms has been unchanged since the beginning of the world?

E. Metchnikoff (I. Mechnikov), in *The Nature of Man: Studies in Optimistic Philosophy* (1903), described an interesting comparison of our disharmony in all areas of science: anatomy, physiology, psychology, sociology, and philosophy. He observed that no rules exist as to how humans are developing anatomically, physiologically, psychologically, socially, or philosophically, except the rules of survival and selection.

Recent studies have proved, in addition to the survival and selection rules of Darwin, sexual preferences in the development of different features. The theory of intelligent design argues for the creational forming of features, meaning an "intelligent designer" created existing forms without any selection and without any changes since the onset of life; denies Darwinism; and is based on a lack of facts about the existence of intermediate life forms and features. However, in science there is no an exceptional choice; neither is there an exceptional explanation of this oversight.

In my practice, I use the theory of E. Mettchnikoff (a.k.a. I. Mechnikov), which poses a lack of certainty in our development that allows for some preferences in choosing signs, norms, standards, and rules for our thoughts and behaviors. The norms of our thoughts and behaviors change according to requirements of the society in which we live and the prevailing authorities. Our normal thoughts and behaviors are revised periodically in the society.

The theory of relativity doesn't exist only in physics. It also exists in social and psychological development. What kind of thoughts can be defined as normal? Society predisposes our normal thought and behavior patterns. If they do not match, for whatever reason (e.g., genetics, poor education, and adaptation to stress), we are talking about illness and mental problems like those listed in the classification of mental diseases in *DSM-IV* and *DSM-V*. Or we think about new ways of living—lifestyles, thoughts, and behaviors. Some practitioners believe there are no norms for human thoughts and behavior, which are disguised under different masks and expressed in the plural roles and games that are only called normal or look normal. However, certain pathological conditions exist that are without a doubt abnormal in nature.

Scientists assume that human thoughts and behaviors are related to DNA's ability to copy the thoughts and behaviors of others people. If this is correct, the disturbance of the ability to copy these features causes mental disorders. The cognitive behavioral method is designed to compensate for and correct this disturbance.

Many psychologists, doctors, and practitioners have developed techniques and systematic recommendations in using this method. The main problem is establishing what's wrong in the patient's belief system and identifying how to modify those beliefs.

The role of the therapist is to help the patient identify in conversation his or her different ways of the negative thinking and replace them with possible alternative modifications. The therapist leads the patient to learn to control the motion of his or her thoughts and to change this incorrect thinking to more functional and logical thinking. Negative ways of thinking are results of distortions in the underlying belief system, or incorrect interpretations of them. Choosing the right correction in the belief system remains the most difficult task in the course of treatment.

Another objective of the cognitive behavioral method is challenging the patient's behavioral pattern, which also has some steps to follow and some obstacles. The play *The Doctor's Dilemma* by Bernard Shaw is an interesting example in literature of the past of choosing the correct principle and action. In the style of science fiction, the hypothetical story introduces to us a doctor who found the remedy for tuberculosis and sought out a limited number of well-known and talented people who suffered from tuberculosis as candidates upon which to test the developed vaccine.

When the list of lucky people was almost full, suddenly a beautiful woman appeared with a request for the doctor to heal and save her husband, who was a brilliant painter and was also suffering from tuberculosis. The discovery of countless defects and loathsome behaviors of this artist presented the doctor with a difficult dilemma, which was solved by considering the value of "genius." In the end, the doctor turned down the last chance of the unfortunate artist.

Instead, the doctor saved the life of his wonderful friend, who was not a skillful doctor but who was a man with a heart of gold. This can be an example of how to make a fair choice in a life situation based on a correct interpretation of the basic belief system. It possibly reflects the idea of the preference for kindness and decency, which are as important as the talent of a doctor, a painter, or a scientist, etc.

Being a good person—this is a personal choice each of us make, and it is not unambiguously predetermined by DNA, as is the case of talent and ability. Does this mean we could be good people and might deserve a special place on the same list as talented people? It seems we might if we wanted to be. Some people think it is better to have talent and different kinds of power, which give a person an exceptional status and control over life, more than is necessary for the survival. For example, some people want money, money, and more money, which sometimes seems to be their absolute and sole purpose.

But the basic beliefs disagree with these people, and they become unhappy, mentally unstable, and ill. They form addictions to drugs and sex because of basic human values that exist in the depths of the soul. These values darken their happiness if they disobey. Therefore, though strange, they condemn this disagreement in themselves and other people.

In my practice, I had one patient who suffered from heroin addiction. Therapy and medications didn't help him until he found on the Internet a girl who came from a very religious family. Her father was a priest.

The girl learned of the tragic flaw of the young man, but after falling in love with him and believing in his ability to change, she invited him to her city, where she lived in a large religious community. After exploring the community, this young man got new knowledge about the meaning of his life. He also received support and love from people in this religious community, where this girl had grown up.

He has since recovered from his drug addiction. He married this girl and eventually got a job. He lives happily with his wife, their beautiful daughter, and their beautiful son in a big house. He never thinks about his past addiction, no matter how hard and stressful his life is at times. This man has kept the core values of love, family, friendship, etc. In certain periods of his life, he had doubts about those values because for a long time he had no evidence of them. He survived drug addiction as a result of the confusion in his belief system. This confusion existed until he met the right girl and joined a congregation with strong values. Then he was able to find a surprising twist to a normal life.

But what can happen to us if we are in such a situation but cannot meet good people who will lovingly and willingly help. Or what if we don't want major changes in our lives or places to live? We will probably attempt to take control of our lives, feelings, thoughts, and actions. Everyone can argue that it is very difficult. But who has tried to take control of his or her life?

Another patient of mine suffered from drug dependence, and when he came to our clinic for therapy, he was on methadone substitution treatment. He spent fifteen years in prison for theft of gold jewelry, which he sold to buy illegal drugs. He justified this with the belief that "all gold merchant are thieves and cheaters," so that sellers of gold deceive buyers and are exorbitant rogues. After spending time in prison, the patient stopped stealing and using illegal drugs, but he was in severe depression. He continued methadone treatment and came to us for psychiatric help.

During the practice of the cognitive behavioral method, some of the patient's symptoms were relieved. With the help of the modification of negative thinking (all-or-nothing; emptiness and uselessness), the patient agreed to apply for a job, and he slowly came to some sort of organized and active life. The patient got employed as a car service driver. He no longer took illegal drugs.

At work, the patient experienced communication difficulties and problems with confidence and trust in people. The correction of his distorted belief system restored him back to a value planted in him by his mother about right and wrong. It helped the patient stabilize the escalation of his symptoms. His mother died from serious illness during his immigration to the United States. The patient immigrated with his father and an older brother when he was only sixteen years old and didn't have the right support or help.

But after treatment, the patient started to believe that his life was going forward and that he could feel like a normal human. By taking advantage of positive interpretations and increasing his own selfrespect, the patient was able to develop relationships with people. He gained confidence in the treatment and the possibility that he could change his life for the better without criminal activity. He restored his self-esteem and his interest in life, and improved his socializing and communication with other people.

As it turns out, this patient has the ability to draw on and has expressed his condition prior to treatment with the following pattern:

We can have all the advantages of being rich and virtuous, talented and morally excellent, healthy and righteous, honorable yet poor, and all deserve to be in the preferred list of important people. Look here for more explanations. All of these benefits don't mean sacrifice, but rather making healthy choices. Because waiting for a favor from fate or helping people who have ignored the basic values (basic belief system) while taking advantage of us—it's all wrong. This makes them more powerful. It gives them the ability to choose for us in life or use the exclusive way to their own gain. That make things worse. The ideal of goodness means anticipating how far it spreads without turning in the opposite direction, namely toward evil and mischief.

In a very interesting movie called *Stalker*, from director Andrey Tarkovsky, a man took several people into Zone, a mysterious and fantastic city, a guarded realm that contained a mystical room where all dreams have to come true and are fulfilled. At the end of this dangerous journey, the man understood that not all dreams are destined to happen and that they can be terrible and fateful. This man's disappointments were staggering because he understood the truth, that he served the ignoble matter. Because of this, his dream to make all people happy without selection was destroyed, and the magic place was liquidated. It is only the proof and conformation of incorrect interpretations of our belief systems.

This is another extreme misinterpretation of the basic belief system, which reflects replacement and confusion with different types of beliefs that support nonbasic values (e.g., style of clothing; preparation of food; celebration of the holidays; observance of traditions, customs, rituals, etc.). It expresses the belonging of people with these general values to groups; the complex and contradictory expressions of religious persuasions are like some of the identities within these groups. (Misinterpretations also exist in different types of religious cults, which are not a topic of discussion here). Interpretation of nonbasic beliefs will cause criticality. The absence of these elements in thoughts also leads to incorrect conclusions and errors that label the practice as unrealistic, unsustainable, and unviable.

Thus, the evolved schema and model of thinking that results from the productive combined efforts of the patient and the therapist have to correspond accurately to the present reality. It is necessary to use in practice both optimistic-positive and realistic-functional thinking. When we have quite a bit of optimistic thinking, we should be concentrated on the positive aspects of facts and events in our lives, work gradually with situations that give rise to negative thinking, and deal with small and big problems, thereby increasing motivation for bright ideas, improving our situations in life, and creating more real reasons and motives for positive iridescent thinking.

Another way to reduce negative thinking emanates from minimum benefits and using comparisons with far worse situations in life, as well as concentrating on small positive developments as good signs for continued progress and replacing negative thoughts with more positive interpretations. As additional assistance, in order to more easily focus on positive interpretations, you must assign positive questions that correspond to the Socratic method. This is a very effective aid for therapists in creating more positive questions for the patient, or for the patient to come up with questions to pose in conversations with himself or herself.

A great inspirational poem written by poet R. Kipling contains an example of changing negative thinking and perception:

If

If you can keep your head when all about you
Are losing theirs and blaming it on you;
If you can trust yourself when all men doubt you,
But make allowance for their doubting too;
If you can wait and not be tired by waiting,
Or being lied about, don't deal in lies,
Or being hated, don't give way to hating,
And yet don't look too good, nor talk too wise:
If you can dream—and not make dreams your master;
If you can think—and not make thoughts your aim;
If you can meet with Triumph and Disaster
And treat those two imposters just the same;
If you can bear to hear the truth you've spoken
Twisted by knaves to make a trap for fools, Or watch the things you gave your life to, broken, And stoop and build 'em up with worn-out tools;
If you can make one heap of all your winnings And risk it on one turn of pitch-and-toss, And lose, and start again at your beginnings And never breathe a word about your loss; If you can force your heart and nerve and sinew To serve your turn long after they are gone, And so hold on when there is nothing in you
Except the Will which says to them: "Hold on!"
If you can talk with crowds and keep your virtue,
Or walk with kings—nor lose the common touch,
If neither foes nor loving friends can hurt you,

If all men count with you, but none too much;
If you can fill the unforgiving minute
With sixty seconds' worth of distance run—
Yours is the Earth and everything that's in it,
And—which is more—you'll be a Man, my son!

Modification of thinking and its replacement by a positive define a new meaning in life. It is the first step in the beginning of change in our lives, or overcoming the symptoms of mental disorder. The next step is to challenge one's behavioral pattern.

Thinking about an action is not the same as taking an action. We should develop a new strategy for our behavior, which once supported our negative or dysfunctional thinking, or in case of disease, its symptoms.

Before we make this "journey," we should clarify for ourselves our ability to balance positive and negative thinking, which are reflected in reality and accurate, verified data.

One person described his perception of his health and other qualities as being similar to a pendulum oscillating and deflecting from the middle of a scale. And our mental health affects how we control this so-called pendulum in our minds, trying to get closer to the golden mean that we cannot achieve.

But if we have negative thinking, we should reexamine its reality and reduce its value in our consciousness. We need to resolve our current problems slowly, step-by-step, splitting large to small, and gradually reducing their amount in each situation respectively and increase our positive reality-based thinking. In case those negative thoughts are real and their resolution is temporarily impossible or not possible at all for some reason, other plans and strategies are necessary: concentrate on positive aspects of our reality, accept those limitations, put up with restrictions, and allow for imagining positive, realistic solutions in the future, which gives us hope.

It is necessary to concentrate on attempts and efforts to improve the situation. We need to accentuate only positive results in our minds. As noted earlier, in some cases it is necessary to start acting a lot harder than thinking about it. Questions, doubts, and errors discourage and hinder our actions. We easily give ourselves and others promises and hear the same from others, but they are far from reality, or our desire to execute them. In the end, nothing changes for the better in our work and lives. Folk wisdom says sow an act, reap a habit; sow a habit, reap character; sow character, reap a destiny.

Also, insightful people say we eat from two dishes during of our life spans: one dish has been cooked by us; the other has been cooked by fate. Our expectations for better changes to our lives or to the mental conditions of patients are like spiders making cobwebs and waiting for flies. In other words, if we are succeeding in our visions, we must be prepared for the gifts of destiny. It requires doing some work before it's time for our well-being and the opportune moment ripen. Then we can expect positive results.

We need to be prepared for our luck and make things happen. Not everything—or practically nothing—comes by itself as a consequence of success or successful predisposition of DNA combinations, without attempts or passive expectations of luck, which is not a single hope in our lives.

One example of how the cognitive behavioral method helped a patient in my practice is very impressive. A ten-year-old boy suffered from post-traumatic stress disorder and displayed the following symptoms: the inability to talk loudly (he whispered); the inability to sleep alone or stay alone in a room; refusal to go to school; and nightmares. This happened when the boy witnessed a crash: parts of a large truck shattered into many pieces, injuring several people who were passing by peacefully along a pedestrian path.

The little boy watched the accident on the road as he strolled with his mother and his sister, who was only a year older. Although the little boy and his family were not injured, he started to experience the above symptoms and was taken for therapy. After the therapist established contact with the boy, who was accompanied by his mother, the therapist taught the boy the cognitive behavioral strategy. The boy learned that this emergency was a very rare case and unlikely to happen again, as well as what else might happen—other events for which the boy should be prepared without overreacting. His concern about his and his family's safety was not an issue at that moment.

The boy was trained in the method of gradual exposure (i.e., every day he gradually increased his previous independent activities and habits) and eventually came back to normal behavior and thoughts: nothing similar or terrible will happen, and it is nothing to fear. After several months, the boy recovered completely and showed remarkable improvement in school, with good grades and good behavior. He also played enthusiastically in soccer games.

A drawing made by a ten-year-old male patient in my practice who suffered from post-traumatic stress disorder.

Like this example, everyone can eliminate unwanted habits with the gradual introduction of the desired skills and new actions.

Before making these changes, it is useful, first, to imagine every little phase of the new behavior. This is a part of behavior modification.

An interesting model for each person can serve as self-control and self-education. An example of this is described in the literary portrait of a writer named Anton Pavlovich Chekhov by another writer named Carney Ivanovich Chukovsky. Chukovsky gave a model personality of the remarkable writer as an illustration of the enormous work for the change; it was a model of the best thinking and behavior based on extraordinary and harmoniously balanced ideals.

A. Chekhov was talented, but he never showed this, remaining among people like everybody else. Chekhov spoke: "True talent always stays in the darkness away from crowd and exhibition." He knew that nobody paid extra attention to ordinary people, but he still preferred evade notice. He said, "No one wants to love in us usual people... But this is wrong..." Chekhov believed that "good manners are not in the fact that you will not spill sauce on the tablecloth, but in the fact that you will not note, if someone else makes this." He called self-education and willpower the responsibility of each noble person, and believed everyone had to develop greatness and self-control of instincts that isn't just an exercise but a duty of every person in the community, since the happiness and progress of humanity depend upon those efforts.

Chekhov hated two basic defects of the average man's soul that seemed to him especially vile: showing outrage above the weak people (roughness, arrogance, swagger, haughtiness, conceit, giving self-airs, and boasting) and exhibiting self-disparaging behavior around strong people (servility, toadyism, excessive pleasing of someone, self-humiliation, and excessive flattery). Chekhov considered that "you realize your nonentity before the mind, beauty, nature but not before the people. Among the people it is necessary to realize own merit." He believed that self-insignificance could be recognized toward beauty, nature, and intellect but that among people everyone is equal and dignified.

Chekhov learned to compromise but not give up his ideals, to cooperate but remain solid and firm in what he believed. He was a master at yielding without being subdued and being lenient without being easily controlled. With delicacy, he never feared offending others if they though to a microscopic degree touched his feelings of respect for himself. He was delicate and polite to others people but never allowed others to treat him any other way. He had great patience and tolerance for others, but he was never selfdefeating, servile, or soft.

According to Chekhov, well-bred people must meet the following conditions:

1. Educated people respect another human personality as an equal. Therefore, they are always lenient. They are flexible, gentle, polite, and cooperative. They don't rebel because of the lost little thing. Living with someone, they do not make from this favor. If they share apartment with someone, they never slam the door when leaving, saying it's impossible to live with someone. They forgive others for noise, and cold, and overcooked meat, and sharpness, and presence of strangers in their dwelling.

2. They are not remorseful and compassionate for cats and dogs and the homeless, but they are worried about other things that are not obvious and cannot be seen with the naked eye. They can't sleep at night in order to help pay the bills of poor student brothers or cloth their own mothers.

3. They respect other people's property and pay their debts on time.

4. They are sincere, upright, and fear lies like fire. They don't tell lies, even in trifles, because lies are insulting for the listener and vulgarizes him in the eyes of that speaker. They do not exaggerate their own roles in anything among people who are poorly informed about them. They do not talk too much or tell every small detail about themselves. They are quiet and respectful to others' ears most of the time.

5. They are not self-humiliating in order to break others into tears, make them feel sorry for them, and cause sympathy in friends. They do not play with others' feelings or on the strings of strangers just to make other take care of them.

They don't say, "Nobody understands me!" or "Nobody gives the prize of two cents for me!" because this is cheap, vulgar, old-fashioned, and fake.

6. They do not rush. They do not pay attention to fake brilliance such as an acquaintance with a celebrity, the handshake of a drunken actor, or the enthusiasm counter in the Salon's reputation. They laugh at the phrase, "I am an important reporter." They do not advertise something cheap as very big. They do not boast about one hundred dollar deals or that they have been allowed to walk in places where others have not. True talents always stay away from fake presentations; they are away from people's eyes in the darkness. As the famous writer Krylov said, an empty cask sounds louder than full.

7. If they have talents, they respect this. They sacrifice for it by rest, women, wine, and fuss. They are proud of their talents. They do not booze with different common people, and acknowledge that their purpose is to be a good influence on them, not bad. Also, they are squeamish (talking about alcoholism).

8. They learn to be esthetical. They can't fall asleep in their clothing, watch walls with cracks and breaks and bed bugs, inhale stuffy air, walk on a splitting floor, or eat from the pot. They try to strengthen and ennoble sexual instinct. They need from the woman not bed, not "horse" perspiration, not mind, or skill to lie without tiredness. They, particularly artists, need freshness, refinement, humaneness, and the ability to be and mother. They are clean, great, sincere, gentle, and creative rather than deceitful, cunning, vulgar, cheap, lying, and dirty. They do not get drunk or smell like closets, because they are not pigs. They drink when they are free, at a convenient time since it is necessary to them "mens sana in corpore sano" because a healthy spirit is in healthy body (talking about alcoholism).

Another very interesting idea is to build a new character as described in a bibliographical book by H. Shtoll about the life and achievements of Heinrich Schliemann (1822-1890), who had an amazing dream to recover ruins of the famous Troy (described by Homer) and finally discovered archeological treasures. H. Schliemann believed that one who has patience is wise and that patience is better than any other kind of strength. He believed that having fortitude, intelligence, and serenity is the best way to reach any goal, and that being reasonable, patient, and calm is necessary also. He believed that happiness is the reflection of the results of one's own accurate thinking and activity. Schliemann encountered the loftiness and tactlessness of one man when he needed money, and he suffered from it. Because of this, Schliemann believed that everyone he helped deserved fair and delicate treatment. In other words, be sensitive and tactfully offer assistance. He believed that no matter how much of a scoundrel his father was, he deserved fair treatment according to the moral laws of all times and people.

Schliemann hated jealousy and games around this in any form, with the exception of "white envy." Yes, but without resorting to dishonest methods, I'd first found out in what he excels, and until then would work hard to overcome own shortcomings, would overpower them and then climb upon the top. He believed in finding what he was doing wrong or not enough of and working hard until he removed mistakes or overcame deficiencies or his poor performances, and he didn't allow them to take precedence. This is the only healthy reaction toward other people's achievements, as opposed to the unhealthy way of destroying the image of the person who had this superiority.

An interesting conclusion appeared in the afterword comments of Sergey Lvov about the novel *Homo Faber,* written by author Max Fisher. He described an idea of this fictional book as a hope that the impeccable scientific logic would help people with the art of creativity to gain a clear point of the view of the modern world, especially the spiritual world of humans, as well as the reality without absolute and perfect schema. Lvov also compared a hero of this book with C. Darwin, who regretted that in the slope of life, he didn't have the time to express himself and enjoy arts. That loss of an interest in arts is equivalent to the loss of happiness.

Lvov also emphasized that human beings need not only financial prosperity but also to know why they seek those materialistic accumulations. Human can't live only on their functional purposes and designations. They need to be full of life. Those comments were regarding a hero of the novel of Max Fisher and based on ideas about technical progress, which doesn't improve the spiritual world of humans. Fisher wrote that technology is a trick, an escape or gimmick with the aid of which some people want to reconstruct and design the world so that there will be no room for feelings and emotions.

The desires of the maniacs of technology are to bring the whole world to useful purposes, to reduce all in the universe to useful activity, and to seemingly force world to serve itself or technology, because they can't cooperate and oppose each other as partners, and can't comprehend or embrace the world. Replacing or leaving with no special values of life, they are powerless to envelop it. Technology is a smart way to escape the resistance of the world, to make it more plain and stereotypical, to destroy the spirit of the alive. Technology is a separation and alienation from the living world.

People who seek only to accumulate can only envy those who leave time for art and enjoy the world in its original form. Omar Khayyam wrote, "You collected a lot of money, miser! But didn't you save time to spend it?"

CHAPTER II

THOUGHTS ABOUT US AND THE WORLD

As example of modification of thought and behavior, I would like to present a diary of a person. He or she will not be named, according to our personal agreement about publishing these records and sharing the thoughts and strategies involved in balancing this person's belief system and achievement of the objective.

This diary reflects analysis that is directed toward the more harmonious means of life, which worked for this person in developing a new personality that was desirable for him or her through modification of thoughts and behavior. However, while not all goals were reached or exceeded to a larger degree, main essential progress was established, as planned.

The notes from this diary are chronological in the order of events and were shortened and edited for spelling, grammar, and clarity for use in this book.

JUNE 1974

Every person represents a complex combination of merits (advantages) and demerits (disadvantages). The central failure of all of humanity is excessive talking (garrulity). And most importantly, the experience of the past generation is not preserved by younger generations in their benefit or advantage. And only after going through their own errors will the next generation confirm this, but it is useless for them to conform.

The second failure is how to be truthful and at the same time fit well into a community.

How do we avoid such a fatal error? Indeed, this creates a peculiar contradiction: in order to hide truth, we must lie and be confident that this is necessary. Because the original is a contradiction, we need to be sure that a lie will not be disclosed; otherwise, people will cease believe to us. If we choose to speak truth, it means we place ourselves at the mercy of circumstances. The entire question, obviously, is who we should trust and who we shouldn't. Logically, we can assume that we can't be absolutely sure, not only about others but also ourselves, and we come to the conclusion that we should believe no one 100 percent. Now it is necessary to demonstrate the following qualities: intuition, ingenuity, deliberation behind deeds, developed tactics, and a certain component of willpower and self-restraint.

Envy is no less terrible of a sin of mankind. Jealousy is horrible, both for the person who is envied and the person who is jealous. Firstly, it is an obstacle to achieving the goal, intrigues, and all sorts of trouble. Secondly, it is the poisoned life of thoughts of someone else's well-being, suffering, and torment without the rest, sleep, and normal activities. The situation for the first is, obviously, the next exit—modesty, lack of bragging, a choice of friends (especially trustworthy people in whom we have confidence), a clear commitment to the plot of enemies and friends, and the ability to be solid in stressful situations.

The advise for the second is a constant struggle with black envy from the consciousness of one's own dignity; a certain confidence in one's own actions; honesty; the awareness of one's shortcomings, without self-humiliation and self-criticism; growing self-respect, greatness, and dignity; increasing self-esteem; faith in the good future; hope for good luck and that everyone will get what they deserve; appreciation of what one is getting at the present time; trying to earn happiness in accordance with one's own capabilities; awareness of the specific provision based on one's own efforts, possibilities, intrinsic worth, and consciousness about one's place in the world; and modesty.

OCTOBER 1, 1974

It's a very stressful period. Who knows? Maybe the hardest part still lies ahead. Life is a struggle and defeats the strong. It is a truth long known. Who can declare that is easy? The best medicine is persistence and time, fidelity to the truth within one's own soul, and faith in self-worth.

However, faith in self-worth is only relative. I am now fretful about several problems:

1. How will I remain fair and just without causing harm to other people?
2. How will I rise above evil?
3. Where can I get strength to overcome adversity and hardship?
4. How will I remain true to myself and not cause inconvenience to people, triumph over unfairness to myself, and guard myself from other people's unfairness?
5. How will I rid myself of vanity, pride, boasting, excessive ambitions, rudeness, unevenness, complacency, egoism, willfulness, and self-assertion?
6. How will I remain critical of myself to preserve the self-confidence?
7. How can I get rid of flatness and extremeness in judgment of others?

8. How will I maintain flexible relationships and preserve dignity, sincerity, and naturalness?

And now I'll try to understand myself and the matter, though the wording and formulations of those questions are somewhat unspecific. The excuse for this is only an immense chaos in my head that is expressing different complex thoughts, which are not dazzling, precise, clear, or logical formulations of thinking, yet.

1. *How will I remain fair and just without causing harm to other people?*

First, I will try to understand what fairness and justness mean.

In my concept, validity of fairness and justness is when a certain balance is achieved between needs, options, and possibilities. I realize that depends on me (my own justness and my own truth to myself and other people) and only in a very small degree on people's justness toward me. At this point, all my statements about fairness have been spontaneous and unconsidered. I lack the clarity and control of my feelings, thoughts, and deeds.

Validity must be proven by actions and confidence in one's own righteousness and not by words. In this case, it is necessary to have tactful respect for people and not act out of the impulse of anger and spite, to think before I act. I should have more indulgence, love, and tenderness for other people. It is necessary often to forgive, to explain something one more time, and to give a second chance. Certainly, it is foolish to try to amend other people or the world, but if there is extreme unfairness, I must be solid and learn to assert myself in rare occasions. If somebody repented, I should forgive and calm this person, even apologize for my behavior. If there is no confidence in my righteousness but circumstances require decisive actions, I must try not to make mistakes, and then without remorse I can look people in the eye and no one will have reason to hesitate in any reproach to me. Most importantly, don't blame yourself too much if this goes wrong. It is necessary to preserve a diplomatic and flexible approach; then habit will be set, and it will become easier with experience.

2. *How will I triumph over evil?*

In my opinion, this is the most difficult question. Someone said that evil is produced within or by stupid or unfortunate people. The only way to keep myself from evil is to avoid the creation of evil (i.e., not allow the possibility to cause evil in me) and avoid unhappy and foolish people who could hurt me or others. But since the issue was raised generally, evil must be fought primarily with evil, which may be caused to another person, despite the fact that this is not always grateful and rewarding.

I believe it is necessary to learn to do good unselfishly only for those who are worthy. Otherwise, my fairness becomes the source of evil (i.e., it will give force and energy to evil, making bad people stronger and more powerful). It also means that I can't be persuasive if I am becoming as bad as those people. What if someone did evil to me? I should not respond the same way. In my opinion, proud contempt must be the most terrible revenge for these people. But sometimes, however, a good man should be forgiven. If the unfairness was a result of a mistake, it is necessary to forgive and forget sometimes, even if this is hard.

This does not include betrayal; betrayal has never been a fine quality of a person, and it in no way can be tolerated. Fighting villainy should be ruthless! I should unmask this person and be merciless, or if this is impossible, then according to the principle of proud contempt, I must simply ignore this. In this case, the main thing is to be confident in your rightness, and if a blunder or error is discovered, it is necessary to preserve a strong spirit and a cool and clear mind to try to correct the mistake and never repeat it again. Nobody is guaranteed against errors. Our main purpose is to recognize them and rightfully acknowledge them.

3. *Where can I find strength to overcome adversity and hardship?*

I have already partially answered this question: only validation of my own blamelessness, purity, and confidence in my own relevance are going to make me strong. But it's not only that. Some people draw their strength from other people, searching for objectivity and approval. This is a very important detail. We often cannot be objective and look for objectivity in other people because only comparison and contrast give us confidence in the correctness of our actions. But it might cause the opposite result. We can help an objective approach to ourselves and other people in this state, when we are not burdened with grudges, praise, and all that prevents us from calmly and sensibly evaluating a situation. Only comparing other people's opinions with our own can give us confidence in the correctness of our thinking and behavior—a clear picture of reality.

However, relying on cold reason and being only calculative and cold minded are not the only strength we need to hope. It shouldn't discard the voice of consciousness, or in other words, our strong belief system, which reflects our hearts, souls, feelings, and intuition in real life. We can see another difficulty is dancing with the danger of being idealistic and again adhere to lofty standards in everything. This forms into a vicious cycle.

We are not ideal creatures and never will be, no matter how hard we try, which is an okay, normal, and realistic outcome in life. We can only concentrate on our efforts and the positive results of these efforts and never be too tired to initiate again and again our goodwill to reach the ideals that replicate our perfect belief system. If we examine a person with an ideal conscience (i.e., by standard equalizing ourselves and our behavior and other people and their behavior), then it is possible to be somewhat objective. Other sources of our strength are self-control, confidence, self-education, will to live, setting accurate goals, endurance, calmness, and assurance in victory and success.

4. *How will I remain myself and not cause inconvenience to other people, triumph over unfairness in myself, and guard myself from other people's unfairness?*

This is also one of the most difficult issues. First, regarding types of unfairness, there are hypocrisy, lies, laziness, envy, rudeness, hastiness, lack of balance and politeness, tactlessness, engaging only in self-interest or profit, etc.

I wrote about garrulity and envy already. Basically, what I want to point out is that a person needs internal liberation, confidence, freedom, and acknowledgment of the natural power of beauty and the meaning of his or her existence that correspond to real reflections of beautiful thoughts and feelings that are in balance with appearance, clothing that dignifies a person without shame, hypocrisy, and wearing masks.

But since thus far I do not represent perfection, I should adhere to this guideline: "It is better not to say anything than to say nonsense."

Of course, I would like to make the same demands of other people, but it's absolutely wrong and unfeasible. Also, it is worthwhile for me, just for a moment, in one second, to break my own rules a little and step back from the very high demands that are produced compulsorily when others reproach and blame me for hypocrisy and double standard behavior; they will cease to respect me. That means I do not have the right to require of others the same rules that I follow, in any case not directly, and neither does anyone else. It doesn't mean we can't be fair to each other when we have been treated well. On the contrary, we should return a fair deed as others deserve. It is simply necessary to know how to place ourselves among other people, since nobody has the advantage in our expense, and use our kindness frequently and without good reason. We should stop being fair to ungrateful and selfish people. But what is to be done if we do not know how to differentiate between a right or wrong person?

Thus let's turn the matter to a person we don't know yet. The main thing in this case is the following strategies: preserving respect; paying attention to first impressions; watching others' manners, laughter, and behavior in unexpected situations; noticing when a person loses some control over him—or herself; and, of course, paying attention to our intuition. It seems to me that every person, whomever he or she may be, is worthy of respect. We should respect all human beings without distinction. This is a tactic that might be unmistakable for everyone.

As for sympathy or dislike, they must only change a little and slightly from the main line of a person's behavior during general communication. For empathy, we require facial expressions to some extent: a softer smile or a sincere look so that the other person will feel the message of our pleasant and warm attitudes. In other words, "You love a little but help more." If the emotion you are feeling is antipathy that is singular, and it is possible to allow ourselves this, don't manifest any negative feelings. Just be polite. If a person performed a deception or a really wrong swindle, then it is simple not to note and to ignore him or her.

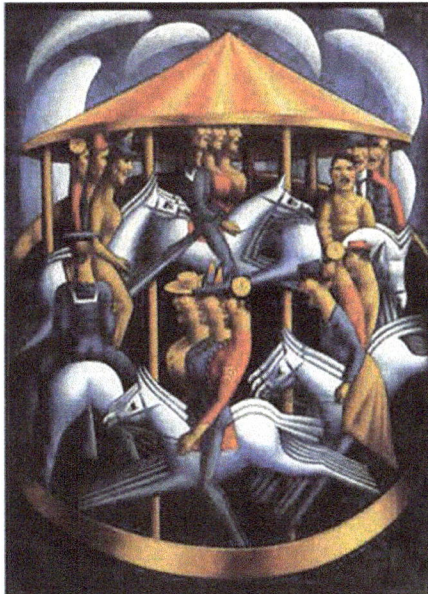

But if conversation leads to a dispute, you should first ask yourself the following question: "If your opponent is worthy of enough intelligence, nobility, honesty, and decency to argue with you, are you worthy of the same?" If not, you should demonstrate tact and dignity, but without hypocritical opportunism, and smoothly change the topic of conversation.

If a person was cruel, then just ignore it. But if it is a situation in which we need to demonstrate sympathy that does not exist in our hearts, then it is better to express by deeds than by words, without compliments, which we don't have in mind.

However, the level of humanity depends on less likable people or different obstacles, which require us to show sympathy in manners we don't typically use in normal circumstances. The best way is, again, to be fair rather than show opposition, and it should be correct to win, at least their respect. Although, frequently in business arrangements and relationships, it isn't enough. It's too much to ask from anyone in this world of contradictions. In some situations, we are required to do everything necessary to solve the problems of life. However, the main purpose must still be noble or very necessary.

Often we have to give in and accept what we don't like. As the saying goes, that's life. Unfortunately, we cannot save a sterile soul; otherwise, it would be impossible to live among people in general. It is important here to show diligence, but what happens or not is another matter. We are all human beings!

Therefore, in order to guard ourselves from other people's indiscretions, we need a lot of strength, moral education, and knowledge of life and people. With the right strategy, it is possible to retreat one's own principles or challenge them if they are not suitable in different time and situations. We don't need to worry that indiscretions of others go unpunished; they can be punished by their own indiscretions at another time. Acknowledgment of this fact might help heal wounds, but maybe not for some people. We are obliged to apply all our knowledge and efforts, be cautious of any stress or dangerous situations, and avoid bad people and their influences. We can use our intuition and good judgment, but we must always be fair to others and act without regretting becoming assertive if they deserve it. Disagreement can be resolved wisely by preserving the opportunity to restore a relationship or a situation to the way it was before the conflict. In other words, don't burn bridges, and find a way back.

NOVEMBER 6, 1974

I have to learn independence and self-sufficiency to fulfill my own needs. This means I must firmly understand my goals, aspirations, feelings, thoughts, and desires, and not try to preempt events or slow down. This means I must take into consideration all objective and subjective facts, as well as the situation.

What's my line in relation to the other?

1. Keep everyone at a distance, but very quietly, discreetly, and of course, naturally.
2. Don't discuss or explain anything in a direct way if it is not vitally necessary. If something is not clear, proceed with caution and wait.
3. Lead the conversation cleverly but also frankly and objectively. View your voice as nice, kind, and wise, always sincere and impartial. Control excessive good and poor feelings. Tell your own opinions unobtrusively, not categorically, and always add, "In my opinion," "I might do it differently, if you want to hear," "As you know," "I think," and "I would have done so or so."

You should have confidence in such behavioral tactics, which are caused by necessity and which will benefit all, though it will require much effort from you. There is no certainty that such tactics are needed all the time. In a good, sincere situation, always answer in the same way, but when met with selfishness and indifference, try to outwardly conform to the same manner.

NOVEMBER 25, 1974

Now it is important to quit selfishness and all the qualities that are not dignified or that make me unworthy for what I strive. I need to strengthen my heart for the possibility of reaching my goals. I have to keep this in mind and not pay attention to every little thing that not in sync with my dignity and honesty in the entire range of human errors and mistakes.

I understand that this is only a dream that never might come true and that what I will become will be a far likeness and pitiful resemblance of that about which I dream. But this dream is not separated from the content of my soul and the natural form of its expression.

I distinguish that my happiness depends on giving happiness and joy to others, which only makes sense as purpose. And I would like the others to give the same to me.

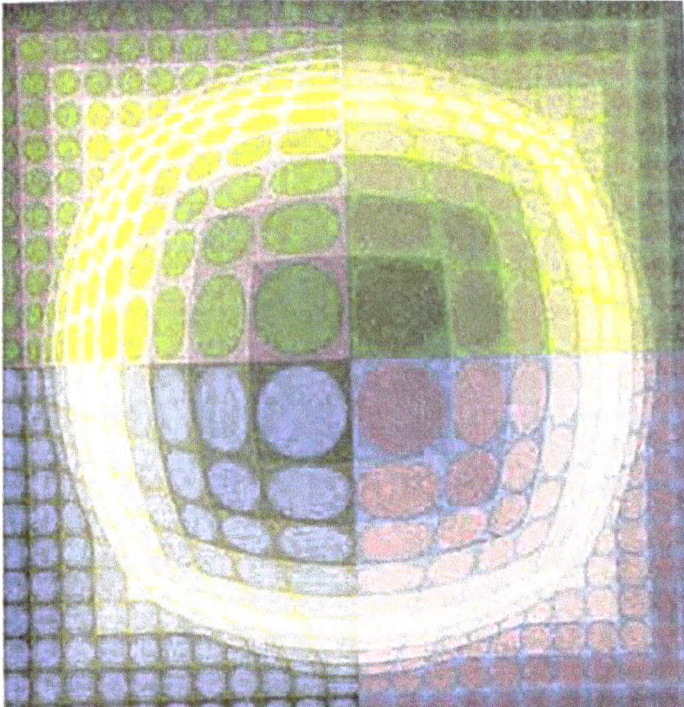

JANUARY 26, 1975

One more year has passed, and a new one is coming. What will it bring to me?

This year was hard and difficult, but I don't think it is all behind me; more hardship is waiting ahead. I desire to define a specific plan and precise direction that is necessary for me to follow.

My main purpose is to make a valuable contribution in the happiness of other people and also to help myself and others discover the truth and magnificent meaning of this beautiful existence.

The means for achieving this aspiration are good studies and work, as a consequence of this good position (but this might never happen since in the name of the same purpose, I might get nothing). Additional aspects are excellent knowledge and the skills to use it; expanding experience; endurance; clear disposition and determination of morality; clarity of thinking; and motivation. I also need to train myself independence in all aspects of life; choose the right schedule; strictly regulate the time; and use all opportunities and options that are wise and fair without turning from my basic purpose.

Ways of gaining of strength are using any tiny possibility to relax (e.g., movies, theater, parties, socializing). In a case where this is impossible, it could be TV, an interesting and distracting book, working alone the house, learning a foreign language, taking in fresh air with long walk, drawing, etc.

My main direction is to be passionate, enthusiastic, and goal directed. If I catch a blue moment, I need to go out and divert myself from all sad and upsetting things using any and all possibilities, options, and choices.

It's almost impossible to predict the future, but I can try to remember one thing: even the attempt to be happy is possible in unfavorable situations. I must not lose optimism, but at the same time I shouldn't shut my eyes to the negative side of life. I must look into reality firmly and without panic or fear, which predict terrible possibilities. I must also be ready for anything, for all unexpected contingencies and dangerous curves of fortune.

I don't have the right to practice self-determination and willfulness in an excessive way. Instead, I have to be independent without complaints (with the exception of extreme situations).

In this fight for goodness, I might draw some actions with negative results for people who deserve it. I don't think I need to be too patient with bad people and wait for justice to come by itself. However, if I punish others, I will be punished also. It's important to arise and go further with all the passion and beliefs that inspired me before.

I need to delineate myself and expand my self-confidence in what I am doing. It's time to end idealization; relate to myself critically, but in an amicable way; care for myself while at the same time working with all my deficiencies, defects, and errors; and relate to myself as a friend. But if it arises, I must scold myself when I am wrong and deserve self-blame, but I should not let it lead to desperation. I should to be objective and fair to myself, and if this is an opposite situation, then I need to lose excessive ambition, quit showing off, be natural, and as sincere as possible. So the skeleton exists; let's hope the flesh will increase. If I believe I can do this, I can build my personality as I want it to be.

January 4, 1975

There is a lot of what is not simple to describe in this diary, and for what? Most important, this is my study, my degree in college. This is my aspiration, and this is my freedom. At least one and a half years left until my graduation. When I graduate the college… I will begin an independent life. It is necessary for me to have knowledge, endurance, self-control, and durability; not to lose my head in anything; and be realistic, calm, and focused on resolving problems.

I need to train myself to independence, even in the small things like cooking, carrying out all household chores, controlling spending, taking care of things and treasuring them more than I do now. I need to learn to be a master of skill and not depend on anybody! I need to behave independently and with dignity. I need to enjoy small things and any possibilities, and always hope for good in the future. I don't have to react to the trifle of life or to one little thing, or be irritable and take everything personally or to heart. This year is the year of my strength test. And it is a pity that it is something that isn't possible to describe or get down on paper everything as it happened in real life. But I don't believe that is necessary.

What I consider necessary to develop and write about are the following qualities:

1. Self-control, calmness, composure, and confidence
2. Thinking before speaking (be quiet mostly and prefer to keep silent)
3. Learning to listen or give the impression that I am listening if I don't want to hear
4. Not keeping things for a long time or putting aside what is possible to do today (today is always more preferable than tomorrow)
5. Not being lazy at all is a must
6. Learning to manage feelings, mimics, gestures, and actions
7. Not showing negative emotions

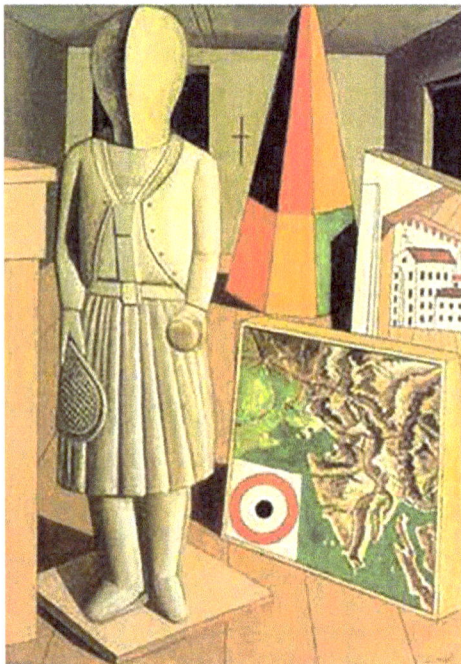

JANUARY 25, 1975

First, I need to be financially and emotionally independent and physically healthy to make my dream come true: to create goodness and progress in my life and in general promote progress and goodness in the world. I need to always remember this direction, no matter how difficult and conflicting life can be in the realization of this. I must think over all my actions to keep balance and fairness in everything, not compromising one goodness for another that could be reached with hard work, self-discipline, patience, a lot of effort, and courage. Then I could serve humanity truly and honestly.

Only the desire to serve others is not enough. I need a lot of strength as well as necessary abilities and qualities, and the knowledge and skills to use them. I need to work hard in implementing any smart ideas in real life; better organize my efforts, time, tasks, and actions; and use better discipline and a structure in my life as a balanced strategy. Certain things are interfering with reaching those goals: laziness, sluggishness, slow pace, inertia, inability to balance my strength. I spend my energy more in unimportant areas and put insufficient efforts toward my real needs; I am absent-minded, forgetful, emotionally unstable, and too talkative, and I put aside the matter at hand for prolonged periods. I don't preserve time or energy in my emotions, make excuses in keeping my things straight and putting off their realizations for a long indefinite amount of time, spend time on unimportant things and emotions, and get up late in the morning.

I need to do certain things to liquidate this imbalance: follow a good diet, slowly and gradually change my habits and lifestyle, as well as organize my tasks and activities better. However, I might also keep myself from dedication to perfect schemas, protect myself from a one-sided attitude, be spontaneous and flexible enough in my schedules, and be able to structure my work and tasks systematically, step-by-step until the end. I should remember that all is good in time; have rest and leisure time with work—planned or unplanned; now allow excess and excessiveness, either in enjoying myself or extreme working; have physical, meditation, and relaxation exercises; keep track of time with respect to my time and the time of other people; keep my duties and obligations to others; distinguish between important and insignificant goals with realistic and good judgment; and develop the ability to miss or lose something small in order to gain bigger challenges, without sacrificing my principles in reaching my main goal.

JANUARY 26, 1975

I understand that until I overcome my weakness, until I control myself and develop willpower, until I strengthen my health, I can't reach my goals and can attain no happiness. Any moral intentions without real support and strength are not attainable.

I should compile a program of minimums and draw my agenda for the accomplishment of my goals. I need more practical aspects of experience: independent ability to do housework, chores, business, and study in real-life situations. All of these are directed toward my experiences in my profession, related science, and way of life in ways that are interesting, necessary, and close to my work and my life situation. I don't need to demonstrate my opinions and explicate myself to others, especially when nobody asks me. My opinions can vary, but my image might remain and stay the same for others even after I have perfected my personality. I need to allow sociability, but without granting permission to access my real personality, with the exception of close friends.

Anyway, I need to be the same: sincere, natural, down to earth, and easygoing. I need to constantly hide my bad mood by smiling more and telling jokes funnily and kindly. My humor needs to be without sarcasm and criticism.

The main goal is to be loving and respectful toward others, and ask the same from others. I can't allow others to offend me and all the more degrade myself without reason, be irritated and sensitive, or even act out in response of any of this.

I need to follow my speech and know why and what I am saying. "It is better not to say anything than to say nonsense."

Until I get enough experience, I should experiment only in uncomplicated occasions and in the simple cases to develop my sense of life and my new strategy. I need to avoid making strong moves and conclusions about how to live my life. One step back, two steps forward; it's the best tactic. I need to think before speaking if I am in a hurry, be clear, and be careful before making statements.

I don't need to display my disagreement directly or any negative opinions, oppositions, or dislikes. I need to dignify myself to others in a fair and honest manner, without playing games or flirting without haughtiness. I must be simple, consistent, persistent, gracious, and modest. I can't rest when I achieve something and stop wanting to continue this work in reaching my goals. I don't need to be distressed about my failure, blunders, and shortages.

It takes discipline and demands that I put myself first and then others. It also demands that I be conscientious and kind, speak less and do more, and be silent and sufficient rather than talking and being useless.

JANUARY 29, 1975

The more I think about myself, the more I am convinced of how negligible I am in my actions and how greedy I am in my desires.

I want this a lot, but I can't definitely declare if I am capable of achieving any of these desires to be strong, fair, and becoming. I only feed myself conveniently by my strong intentions, my attempts to place actual targets that are without any obvious result. And this could last forever. However, time has no patience for this. Every minute is priceless in the long run of my finite life span. From now I declare the following:

1. Take care of time. Every moment is precious.
2. Be loyal to your own principles, no matter what. My principles are as follows:
   a. Only in exceptional and extreme occasions may I excuse myself from the release of truth. Try to live so

you can avoid having to lie. Be fair to yourself and to other people.

    b.   Be aware of my own dignity and the dignity of others.

    c.   Be natural and spontaneous.

    d.   Strive for all kinds of beauty.

    e.   Do not betray friends and loved ones.

    f.   Believe in love, friendship, and happiness.

    g.   Insist everything is possible and that even impossible means to achieve goals through hard work and dedication.

    h.   Show respect and appreciation for my parents.

    i.   Assist people in distress.

    j.   Try to be kind, especially to those who deserve it.

    k.   Be honest, noble, and decent to those who meet those requirements.

    l.   Be merciless to those who create evil, lies, hypocrisy, betrayal, etc.

3. Patience and work are my left and right arms.
4. Believe everything and everyone, but be observant.
5. Notice everything without noticing.
6. Silence is golden—the word, silver (talk without disclosing and explaining).
7. Make critical comments kindly and deliberately, without unnecessary and offensive tones.
8. Diplomacy is the arms of the strong.
9. Politeness is a privilege of kings.
10. Cleanliness to a guarantee of health.
11. Everything that shouldn't happen is all for the better.
12. Forget offense, but remember the lesson in the right moment.
13. Forgive not recalling; be tolerant of shortcomings.
14. Consider every moment of life as happiness.

FEBRUARY 9, 1975

Already some time has passed and results have begun to appear. Success is dazzling and making me so blind that I have become numb in unhappiness and difficulties. If I stop continuing my achievement, I will immediately degrade and return to my previous point quickly. These thoughts are limited and have almost stopped me from feeling happy in the present moment. It's almost disappointing and less exciting than I expected. All those results don't surprise me or make me feel proud of myself because they don't come suddenly without warning in the form of pleasant gifts from my luck and fortune.

I believe I need to meet success as a necessary conclusion of my efforts and work to dignify myself and others, and be glad at small things mostly. Only patience is helping me to attain everything. When I am flattering and praising myself, I shouldn't forget my deficiencies and failures. When I disregard myself, I need to remember my successful moments in life.

FEBRUARY 19, 1975

I already thoroughly wrote about what I should do. I can add this: if I observe the short period of time I've been doing these things, I may conclude I am doing fine.

I also state the following things:

1. I am already close to the point where I will be capable to evaluate and judge without any approval or help but my own that I am the creator of my own destiny and able to justify my faults and merits, my gains and errors.
2. I understood that my happiness is a goal-directed duty for progress, and I delight in this creative work.
3. My parents are my main support as well as my best friends, and the finest way is loving them as they deserve, without paying excessive attention to their faults and errors.

4. I know how necessary it is to always delight in life in any circumstance, without forgetting about my honor, conscience, and soul-searching experience.

5. I need to believe in any possibility of love, friendship, and happiness without considering and suggesting difficulties of their maintenance and preservation for the long term.

6. I should be consistent in observing my principles without the burden of small deviations that compromise my goals and beliefs. I should also predispose my assurance in my own dignity and calm my consciousness of my self-worth and confidence.

7. I should to question my conscience about truthful and immoral issues before I make any strong move or decision that will not convey my regret and remorse.

FEBRUARY 22, 1975

I have felt like I need to systemize my point of view on the world and present that system for a long time. I've passed through all the extreme feelings of ecstasy and disappointment and have been in all the opposing and contrasting directions with my emotions: admiration, wonder, disregard, and doubt. And, after searching for the truth, I am nevertheless convinced and admit that the best system is the present system in our society, despite the contradictions, disharmony, and misbalance around the world, which for some reason I have difficulty accepting. But the basic principles I recognize with all my heart. Even I deny and dismiss of some of the sides of the present system, but I still can't be wise enough to propose another balanced replacement.

But I can't always live with flow without any changes to my thinking and conscience. I can't allow myself to be that irresponsible and immature person. I must add that it is important to find and get experience from life examples, events, and reality. The main thing that would be desirable for me is to affirm humanism, honesty, hard work, and beauty in my life. I disapprove of some methods and forms in the present system. But I am certain about people who create injustice and disagreement and critics who can't stand upon the high standards they set for others by using double standards (what is allowed for them is not allowed for others) and those who distort their own and others' principles in name of freedom of disharmony, uncertainty, and confusion in present society. If I observe balanced and harmonious principles strictly according my beliefs, I will be named naive, a fool, a hypocrite, or retarded. If I intend to follow my principles with my mind and my heart, there will be no harm or damage to anybody. Let me reiterate it in a different way: principles don't have to conflict with other people. Only this is effective and real in the present existence of truth and the maintaining of perfect balance. If they are in conflict, I will be wrong unintentionally. But what can I do? I require a lot of moral and physical strength and effort to carry out this! Most importantly, I can't allow myself to be relaxed or indulgent with losing the points of the truth. I need a lot of learning, reading, watching, experiencing, living real life, and experimenting in order to serve this truth. I need to oblige myself rather others, not rest in weakness or helplessness, and do a lot of thinking...

APRIL 23, 1975

For very long period, I didn't take time to make notes and didn't express myself in my diary. However, what did happen during this period of time in my consciousness?

It began to be more easy to live. It is more interesting. I have purpose—serving to progress. I have relatives and friends. My personal life somehow blended into the background. Maybe it's for the better...

I still need to accomplish a lot of prospects. Many things to overcome and alter in the future wait. I feel much stronger and struggle with feelings and obstacles that I'll survive in general. However, I can't be stronger than circumstances. I am confident to serve for fairness, love, happiness, but I don't have enough experience and abilities to be any of this yet. Sometimes my conscious forces my unconscious, abilities, and situations forward to a far-out distance. Most importantly, I don't have to prove myself to anybody, including myself. Only I need to go further without turning away from my success.

What do I plan in the future?

1. Graduate the college.
2. Become a good specialist.
3. Learn a foreign language.
4. Continue to work at the study of various sciences besides my profession.
5. Get my own family based on love with a good person.
6. Have two children.
7. Take care of my parents, relative, and friends.
8. If it is possible, study more serious science;
9. Continue with self-education, constantly improving myself to become polite, kind, good-looking, healthy, interesting, and a family person who never loses heart and does not quail.

June 20, 1975

I didn't write in my dairy for two months. My mood is down a little. The thoughts constantly torment me: for what purpose do I live? What defines my sense of life? What do I do that is particularly good and honest? Am I right or wrong, etc…?

In life I have made many mistakes, some of them irreparable. I pretend to have high moral value. But am I worthy to try them? I still need to struggle for fine qualities within myself and in the imperfect surrounding world, qualities that require willpower, self-control, and resistance to weakness and melancholy.

JUNE 1, 1976

I am a step away from independent life. All my honest, moral, and noble ideas are mostly illusions, and majority proved to be not well-off. I have become a more realistic, common, and average person who is doing all the things that others are doing without thinking about noble purposes. People blame me for being impractical and constantly requiring my parents' support in almost everything, as I am useless and a dreamer. I couldn't argue this yet, but if I concentrate maximally on my efforts to make everything that my dream requires possible, I might succeed. It's terrible that I despise mostly everything without considering the right replacement.

I am afraid to be accessible to others or to be a wounded by injustice. I greatly expect purity and loveliness in my own and others' intentions. Sometimes I find myself spiteful and tough. Sometimes I feel vulnerable and fragile. Sometimes I am afraid of the struggle and the consequences of this great effort. Sometimes I feel pity for bad people and doubt what I can do that is appalling for them. Do I have the right to do anything? Am I justified to watch terrible things happening? My life is complete unfairness: I get everything generously when I consider that I do not deserve it. Then it is meager when I hope I deserve it, and I get nothing. I want to reach some clarity and establish real progress.

CHAPTER III

OUR SYSTEM OF VALUES

I cannot present a more difficult task than to define our system of values, which we consider to be important at all times to follow truthful human laws. We have developed the present forms of existence that became absolutely essential for the human race to function, and that reflect common human canons and values, which are defined by present societies. And it has worked in a mystical way through the centuries. Present human democracy is result of the constant change of society, which is based on basic beliefs and values that keep peace, prosperity, progress, and salutary changes for all people of the planet, since the basic religious laws are accepted and followed in one way or another in different countries.

Since ancient times, our belief system among people has been represented and preserved in sacred texts like the Torah, the Bible, the Koran, etc., which have had the most important influence on our lives.

The following list is made up of laws with some of the exact words from those religious treasures:

- "You shall not make yourself carved image..."
- "Six days shall you work...but the seventh day...you shall not work..."

- "Honor your father and your mother, so that your days will be lengthened upon the land…"
- "You shall not kill."
- "You shall not commit adultery."
- "You shall not steal."
- "You shall not bear false witness against your fellow."
- "You shall not covet your fellow's house."
- "You shall not covet your fellow's wife… nor anything that belongs to your fellow."

It is evident that all these laws reflect the Ten Commandments, which humanity has attempted to follow for thousands of years in many countries.

There are other interesting computations:

- "If a man shall seduce a virgin who was not betrothed and lie with her, he shall provide her with marriage contract as his wife. If her father refuses to give her to him, he shall weigh out silver according to the marriage contract of the virgins."
- "You shall not taunt or oppress a stranger, for you were strangers…"
- "You shall not cause pain to any widow or orphan…"
- "When you land money, my people, to the poor person who is with you, do not act toward him as a creditor; do not lay interest upon him…"
- "You shall not curse a leader among your people…"
- "Do not accept a false report, do not extend your hand with wicked to be a venal witness. Do not be follower of the majority for evil; and do not respond to a grievance by yielding to the majority to pervert (the law). Do not glorify a destitute person in his grievance…"
- "Do not pervert the judgment of the destitute person in his grievance. Distance yourself from a false word; do not execute the innocent or the righteous, for I shall not exonerate the wicked. Do not accept a bribe, for the bribe will blind those who see and corrupt words that just. Do not oppress a stranger; you knew the feelings of the stranger, for you were strangers…"
- "Six years shall you sow your land and gather in its produce. And in the seventh, you shall leave it untended and unharvested, and the destitute of your people shall eat, and the wildlife of the field shall eat what is left…"

- "Six days shall you accomplish your activities, and on the seventh day you shall desist…"
- "Three pilgrimage festivals shall you celebrate…during the year."
- "When person will sin unintentionally from among all the commandments…that may not be done, and he commits one of them…shall bring…unblemished…as a sin-offering…"
- "You shall not steal, you shall not deny falsely, and you shall not lie to one another. You shall not swear falsely…"
- "You shall not cheat your fellow and you shall not rob; a worker's wage shall not remain with you overnight until morning. You shall not curse the deaf, and shall not place a stumbling block before the blind…"
- "You shall not commit a perversion of justice: you shall not favor the poor and shall not honor the great; with righteousness shall you judge your fellow."

- "You shall not be a gossipmonger among your people; you shall not stand aside while your fellow's blood is shed... You shall not hate your brother in your heart; you shall reprove your fellow and do not hear a sin because of him. You shall not take revenge and you shall not bear a grudge against the members of your people; you shall love your fellow as yourself..."

- "Do not profane your daughter to make a harlot, lest the land becomes lewd, and the land becomes filled with depravity."

- "In the presence of an old person shall you rise and you shall honor the presence of a sage..."

- "If your brother becomes impoverished and means falter in your proximity, you shall strengthen him-proselyte or resident-so that he can live with you. Do not take from him interest and increase... and let your brother live with you. Do not give him your money for interest... If your brother becomes impoverished with you and is sold to you; you shall not work him with slave labor..."

- "Whoever smites a person, according to the testimony of witnesses shall one kill the killer, but a single witness shall not testify against a person regarding death."

- "You shall not accept ransom for the life of a killer who worthy of death, for he shall surely be put to death. You shall not accept ransom for one who fled to his city of refuge to return to dwell in the land... You shall not bring guilt upon the land in which you are, for the blood that was spilled in it, except through the blood of the one who spilled it. You shall not contaminate the Land in which you dwell..."

- "Every daughter who inherits an inheritance of the tribes... shall become the wife of someone from a family of her father's tribe, so that everyone...inherit the inheritance of his fathers. An inheritance shall not make rounds from a tribe to another tribe, for the tribe...shall cleave every man to his own inheritance..."

- "I instructed your judges at that time, saying, "Listen among your brethren and judge righteously between a man and his brother or his litigant. You shall not show favoritism in judgment, small and great alike shall you hear; you shall not tremble before any man…"
- "You shall not add to the word that I command you, nor shall you subtract from it, to observe the commandments…"
- "… You shall safeguard and perform them, for it is your wisdom and discernment in the eyes of the peoples, who shall hear all these decrees and who shall say, 'Surely wise and discerning person is this great nation!'…"
- "Only beware for yourself and you greatly beware for your soul, lest you forget the things that your eyes have beheld and lest you remove from your life, and make them known to your children and your children's children…"
- "You shall observe…decrees and…commandments that… command you this day, so that… will do you good to you

and to your children after you, and so command you that will prolong your days on the Land… for all the days."

- "You shall do what is fair and good… so that it will be good for you…"
- "You shall cut away the barrier of your heart and no longer stiffen your neck…who does not show favor and who does not accept a bribe. He carries out the judgment of orphan and widow, and loves the proselyte to give him bread and garment. You shall love the proselyte for you were strangers…"
- "At the end of seven years you shall institute a remission. This is the matter of the remission: Every creditor shall remit his authority over what he has lent his fellow; he shall not press his fellow or his brother, for he has proclaimed a remission… You may press the gentle; but over what you have with your brother, you shell remit your authority. However, may there be no destitute among you…"
- "If there be a destitute person among you, any of your brethren in any of your cities… you shall not harden your heart or close your hand against your destitute brother. Rather, you shall open your hand against destitute brother to him; you shall lend him his requirement, whatever is lacking to him. Beware lest there be a lawless thought in your heart, saying, 'The seventh year approaches, the remission year,' and you will look malevolently upon, your destitute brother and refuse to give him—then he may appeal against you… and it will be a sin upon you. You shall surely give him, and let your heart not feel bad when you give him, for in return for this matter…"
- "For destitute people will the Land… You shall surely open your hand to your brother to your poor and to your destitute in your Land."
- "You shall not prevent judgment, you shall not accept a bribe, for the bribe will blind the eyes of the wise and make just words crooked. Righteousness, righteousness shall you pursue, so that you will live and possess the Land…"

- "And you shall not erect for yourselves a pillar…"
- "You cannot place over yourself a foreign man."
- "And he shall not have too many wives, so that his heart not turns astray; and he shall not greatly increase silver and gold for himself. It shall be that when he sits on the throne of his kingdom, he shall write for himself… copies… It shall be with him, and he shall read from it all the days of his life… to observe all the words…"
- "…so that his heart does not become haughty over his brethren and not turn from the commandment right or left, so that he will prolong years over his kingdom…"
- "…When you come to the Land…you shall not learn to act according to the abominations of nations."
- "Innocent blood shall not be shed in the midst of your Land… for then blood will be upon you."
- "You shall not move a boundary of your fellow, which the early ones marked out, in your inheritance that you shall inherit…"
- "…If a false witness stands against a man to speak up spuriously against him, then the two men /and those/ who

have the grievance shall stand before…the judges who will be in those days. The judges shall inquire thoroughly, and behold the testimony was false testimony; he spoke up falsely against his fellow. You shall do him as he conspired to do to his fellow, and you shall destroy the evil from your midst. And those who remain shall hearken and fear; and they shall not continue again to do such an evil thing in your midst. Your eye shall not pity; life for life, eye for eye, tooth for tooth, hand for hand, foot for foot."

- "… when you go out to the battle against your enemy, and you see horse and chariot—a people more numerous than you—you shall not fear them…"
- "… Who is the man who has built a new house and has not inaugurated it? Let him go and return to his house, lest he dies in the war and another man will inaugurate it. And who is the man who has a vineyard and not redeemed it? Let him go and return to his house, lest he dies and another man will redeem it. And who is the man who has betrothed a woman and not married her? Let him go and return to his

house, lest he dies in the war and another man will marry her."

- "... Who is the man who is fearful and fainthearted? Let him go and return to his house, and let him not melt the heart of his fellows, like his heart."
- "... If a man will have two wives, one beloved and one hated, and they bear him sons, the beloved one and the hated one, and the firstborn son is the hated one's; then it shall be that on the day that causes his sons to inherit whatever will be his, he cannot give the right of the firstborn to the son of the beloved one ahead of the hated one, to give him the double portion in all that is found with him; for he is his initial vigor, to him is the right of the firstborn."
- "If a man marries a wife, and comes to her and hates her, and makes a wanton accusation against her, spreading a bad name against her, and he said, 'I married this woman, and I came near to her and I did not find signs of virginity on her.' Then the father of the girl and her mother should take and bring proofs of the girl's virginity to the elders. 'I gave my daughter to this man as a wife, and he hated her. Now, behold he made a wanton accusation against her, saying "I did not find signs of virginity on your daughter" but these are the signs of my daughter!' And they should spread out the sheet before the elders of the city. The elders of the city shall take that man and punish him. And they shall fine him..."
- "But if this matter was true—signs of virginity were not found on the girl—then they shall take the girl to the entrance of the father's house..."
- "If a man will be found lying with a woman who is married to a husband..."

- "If the man will be found lying with a virgin girl who is betrothed to a man, and a man finds her in the city and lies with her… the girl because of the fact that she did not cry out in the city and a man because that he afflicted the wife of his fellow; and you shall remove the evil from your midst."
- "But if it is in the field that the man will find the betrothed girl and the man will seize her and lie with her, only the man who lies with her shall die. But you shall do nothing to the girl, for the girl has committed no capital sin, for like a man who rises up against his fellow and murders him…"
- "When a camp goes out against your enemies, you shall guard against anything evil."

63

- "You shall not turn over to his master a slave who is rescued from his master to you. He shall dwell with you in your midst, in whatever place he will choose in one of your cities, which is beneficial to him; you shall not taunt him.
- "There shall not be a promiscuous woman among the daughter…and there shall not be promiscuous man among the sons…"
- "…You shall not bring a harlot's hire or the exchanges…for any vow, for both of them are an abomination…"
- "You shall not cause your brother to take interest of money…"
- "When you make your fellow a loan of any amount, you shall not enter his home to take security for it. You shall stand outside; and the man to whom you lend shall bring the security to you outside. If that man is poor, you shall not sleep with his security. You shall return the security to him when the sun sets and he will sleep in his garment and bless you; and for you it will be an actofrighteousness…"
- "You shall not cheat a poor or destitute hired person among brethren, or a proselyte who is in your Land, or one who is in your cities. On that day shall you pay his hire; the sun shall not set upon him, for he is poor, and life depends on it; let him not call out against you … for it shall be a sin in you."
- Fathers shall not be put to death because of sons, and sons shall not be put to death because of fathers; a man should be put to death for his own sin."

All of the quotations listed, in one way or another, support the existence of features, regulations, and traditions in our community that have unconsciously been observed by people throughout the centuries and that are reflected in science, art, religious conversions, etc. Some people may agree with this, and some may not. It depends on their families' edification and varies from one community to another.

We know unconsciously how to behave because we acquire through the milk of our mothers some canons of religious beliefs that reflect people's norms and rules without us acknowledging past realities, which have been accepted without knowing their sources. Without a doubt, this predicts and predisposes a community's requirements to our norms of behavior and is what causes these norms to be established in our mental condition. This influence appears as feelings of guilt, emptiness, worthlessness, etc. We can name many shades of the different emotions that reflect our thoughts, which originate from beliefs we acquired in our childhoods and the printed structures of our communities and families at that time and that are left in our consciousness.

Does this mean we need to overlook our basic belief system and scorn everything that interferes with our happiness and prosperity to be free from all responsibilities and guilt? It's not as simple as it seems! We learn to enlarge the boundaries and freedom in our choices of the belief system according to biological, juridical, general humane, and other rules and laws.

All those who were deprived for one reason or another, who lack in some degree any kind of appropriate and adequate education (including self-education), or who replace observing customs and traditions without following basic values or religious culture face serious problems in their communities; create trouble for others (those who observe spiritual culture, rules, and the values of society); produce imbalance, confusion, and chaos; and are responsible for hurting many other innocent people. People who lack basic values also include patients with mental illnesses who use their system of values in error as a result of poor judgment and insight.

Therefore, psychological treatment needs to be different, depending on the group of people—correction of behavior and, if possible, thinking (correction of basic essential beliefs and values) for one group, and healing of wounds for those who became victims of the imbalance that the first group created.

In my experience and personal observation, the majority of people follow basic beliefs and values 60-70 percent of the time, because 100 percent is not possible in order for them to keep making living and surviving, overcoming all circumstances and obstacles that affect their lives. Another group of people make bad choices and mistakes when using their belief system; often this group is not psychologically healthy.

Accordingly, all the people who rate below 50-60 percent adherence to their belief system can enroll in the second group; the rest who follow their belief system above that percentage can count themselves among the first group.

Discrepancy in observing one's own belief system (less 100 percent) leads to distortions of our beliefs, thoughts or behavior that display feelings of guilt, shame, remorse, etc.

All those rules apply to mentally healthy people, who can fall into depression or other mental conditions that normally disappear after six months and less. All conditions that connect to conflicts with our system of the values and disharmony in our belief system and last longer than six months can pass into pathological states and cause mental problems and diseases that are reflected in abnormal functioning.

To avoid the passage of these states into mental disease, it is necessary to use the cognitive behavioral method, which can be helpful and rewarding. The cognitive behavioral method can be useful for mental disorders in different stages, and the results depend upon the severity of the mental dysfunctions and conditions.

There are other gradations during the treatment of pathological conditions and diseases besides those indicated above: people with intelligent and well-developed psychological function and people with undeveloped psychological function and half-educated psychological features; however, there can be other gradations inside both groups.

Both groups have different difficulties and special features in treatment. The first group, those with intelligent and well-developed psychological function, can have different kinds of irrational thinking that seem logical at the first sight. The second group, those with undeveloped and half-educated psychological features, can suffer from lack of adequate information, education, and experience in logical thinking.

The first group reflects different kinds of distortions of a normal range and unusual pathological conclusions that display dysfunctional thinking and behavior. It is very difficult to oppose or contradict and sometimes impossible to convince them of the opposite of their beliefs because that group is very determined in their own sources of information, experiences, and confirmation of authorities they chose previously. They can't easily believe other explanations that differ from already accepted and convenient explanations, no matter the evidence.

The second group tends to trust logic and reasoning less and comprehend the cognitive modifications less because they can't follow complicated conceptions or acknowledge simplifications of the concepts that do not render the essential modification of thinking. But this group easily confirms authorities and better responds to modifications of behavior—all modifications, which gives obvious and evident results.

At first sight, this seems like an insoluble and difficult task. However, if we apply step-by-step corrections and control the patients' thinking and behavior, according to the cognitive behavioral method, we can modify and improve thinking and behavior in both groups with differences in periods of application, provision of the hard work, and appropriate, persistent efforts.

Thus, the question arises: how do we know that all the information we are using is truthful and correct? This question relates to all scientific research and information in our lives that question the validation of a larger number of facts and data: any hypothesis (suggestion) becomes more real and precise if it has more verification in practice, which is supported by experiments in real-life situations.

The facts can decline some authoritative conceptions and rules in communities; it is then appropriate to present the careful explanations and compromised modifications to express more flexibility and tolerance than are in the present disharmonious opinions, which need detailed study and acknowledgment by authorities.

Effectively, we can use a scale from zero to one hundred to verify and authenticate our information. On this scale we can note the probability of facts and their conformation in real life, corroborating them with our own and other people's experiences, which can decrease the number of errors and mistakes.

The sources of correct information are no less important. Some scientific data are only empty speculations and fabrications poorly conformed in pseudoscientific experiments, while other facts that are derived from real-life experiences, even from ancient times, and are without evident data of science but are adjusted by practice can be more useful. Moreover, it is important is to distinguish inaccuracies in both categories of information. This means that nothing can be 100 percent accurate, and it is important to commensurate constantly, revising new data and facts to conform our own and other people's experiences.

This approach in the evaluation of correct information helps prevent development of paranoia and fears and disturbances in behavioral patterns, and improves adaptation, increases tolerance to stress, and maintains more adequate reactions in different situations.

When conducting modification, it is also important to observe and respect a person's personal beliefs errors, which do not interfere substantially with functioning and don't change the condition of the person who is the subject of the cognitive behavioral method. Finally, the purpose is to help improve the functional condition and challenge pathological symptoms without changing all imperfections and inaccuracies. Challenging the personality is not a realistic task and depends on the compliance and promptness of each person in his or her desire to change his or her personality, taking into account the person's age and level of psychological awareness of all the potential consequences. All of the theses listed earlier, which took root in the Torah, Bible, Koran, and other sources, influence our reality firmly and unnoticeably.

Many examples proved the thesis about idealizations and leaders.

Nobody can be perfect or 100 percent right, including our leaders, teachers, theorists, and also priests. That fact is supported by many instances from past and present experiences.

All people rest one day a week and celebrate holidays as requirements of religious scripts. Most people give respect and honor to their parents, which inspires and makes the generation determined to give birth to the children and build new families in immeasurable efforts and sacrifices for future generations, refusing joy, their own peace, and their own needs. In spite of the law in which the future generation denies the previous generation, which represents competitions and contradictions between the generations, the guidelines of the religious beliefs are in balance and regulation. Natural laws precede one generation by another, respecting needs of the older generation and building the healthy, young, and successful population of the future. It is very unreasonable and unfair to underestimate the importance of the proceeding phenomena of respect of one generation by another. This is a most imperative mistake in the development of communities and a deviation from basic religious beliefs and human values.

Famous and valuable contributions have been made in the development and prosperity of societies, science, arts, technology, etc., by old and ancient generations and also by young populations, and it is priceless. It is obvious and unquestionable that the fact exists: there have been some unspeakable degradations in all generations that produce doubts in old experiences and ignorance of young geniuses that lead to an underestimation of old people's role in assisting the future and represses young people's inclinations toward progress and advancement, which can harm the development of the society.

It is important to see roots and origins of past and present evidences of progress and to carefully estimate the future predispositions in the movement of society.

Wars have existed throughout the centuries in religious and unreligious societies, as well as killing of human beings, which has interfered with people's interests and progress within a definite period of time, finds justification even in religious scripts. And these remain most contradictive and very sensitive part of humanity's existence in all periods of the time, in spite of definitions that forbid killing in certain parts of religious scripts and religious beliefs.

It is important that nobody judge or condemn innocent, defenseless people without substantial and credible evidence that is made up of strictly objective facts when dealing with death or the death penalty. Bad examples are the terrorist suicidal bombers that carry a death sentence for innocent people, or also some political leaders' actions. Only justice or equal battle in a battlefield can justify killing in certain parts of religious scripts.

If the killing of a human being happened as a result of a wrong judgment of court or as the result of inequitable war, humanity is still responsible for this and will sooner or later face the judgment of society. There is no innocence because of absence of power or rightness under the leading authority. It is a logic of existence and equality of rights for every person among people. There should be no preference because of multiple and numerous unjustified expressions of support by the crowd. Only humanism and democracy that are based on reason take preference in the justification to take human life.

It defines that no matter if someone wants or doesn't want it, balance and justice have the right to take a lead toward success and to the top. The land rightfully belongs to progressive and creative people in the end, despite the ambitions and proclamations of any group who uses positions of force and injustice to make claims on any land. Humanity is no longer only the numerous wild crowds that have obeyed a small group of people with power. The physical, intellectual, moral, and technological perfections define priorities and equal collaboration, which allow a great amount of people to live their lives in the best way. The individuals and people of different cultures maintain equal and unequal conditions. They have tendencies to live their own ways; they want and deserve to establish worldwide progress.

Another main value of humanity is the dignifying of the sexual instinct and developing the manifestation of appropriate sexual behavior that reflects more alive, realistic, and humanistic forms and appearances. The families and relationships that are based on love, respect, mutual agreement, and equality for both sides that conclude freedom are the center of the scenery of many phenomena, events, considerations, discussions, and debates in the modern world. The relationships exist in forms that are mostly concordant and functioning under religious descriptions, except for some very rare forms that contradict the basic forms and require careful individual approach in every occasion but not censure and reprimand in the society.

Divorces and polygamy in relationships between men and women became reasonable in regulations of equal rights for both sides. And lately, women play a large role and have proved their valuable contributions in different areas of the development of culture, science, politics, and the economy. Those reflect the degree of the emancipation of women, which continues to be strengthened and helps to maintain and establish general human progress. It proved that uncultivated and uneducated women cannot raise many intellectual males to develop and fortify our economy, science, arts, etc.

It is impossible to regulate imbalance in the unremitting and vigilant desires of the male population to have sex, without concordance in the female population.

Despite biological differences between genders, this leads to a huge contradiction and complicated resolution of basic tendencies for the sake of survival and reproduction, and evolution and selection in the physical and moral development of the human race, which builds of circumstances of happiness of the entire world. And this is incomprehensibly difficult to achieve in many deviations of basic religious canons and the necessary derogations.

Certainly, humanity must learn how to revise our basic values without extraordinary or extreme deviations from main sacred principles, return to the more effective old tendencies, and take into account tendencies of the modern times. Surely also, the human race should learn diet restrictions, both in eating and sex, especially if sex is not related to reproduction or other circumstances. We can't use sex intensively for the purpose of profit or influence in politics or any areas besides the main purpose of sex—reproduction, health, inspiration, etc.—without destroying our communities and breaking the religious foundation and rules of our societies.

We can't thoughtlessly leave children without the harmonious influence of a healthy family and grow legalized prostitution in unhealthy marriages. There may be a regulation of child support for children, but it does not support divorced women, especially in instances when a spouse initiated the divorce without substantial reasons. So how about the approach of supplying a small, reasonable amount of financial support for the poorer divorced spouse instead of the big fine lawyers deliver? We need to be reasonable about investing a huge amount of money on the unhappiness of children of divorced families and stop the institution of marriage from being corrupted, as well our ideals. It might be useful to set longer terms for making the decision to marry for couples, especially after divorce, and give less sexual freedom and a larger reprimand of society to the male population.

We can't decide the fate of children only according to sparse evidence and not investigate the doubtful cases of unreasonable accusations of spouses dealing with parental rights and custody. We also can't exaggerate the rights of children and raise little monsters that know well how to hurt their parents and make life a living hell for them. All members of society deserve equal rights and validity in meeting their own needs and happiness without extremes in the judgment and action for both the children and the parents. We need to balance needs and possibilities according family income and other family traditions of multicultural communities, which can't be decided without the help of a healthy family or supplying all kids with the same treatment, or setting high financial standards for all families.

It seems reasonable to educate and instruct young men not only how to use protection and wear condoms during sex but also to acquire a healthy awareness of respect and dignity for their sexual partners—women—and to be more selective besides their physical appearance. We should train them not to blindly follow instinct and to confirm their feelings and manage them without damaging their own psychological and physical health.

It might be sensible to create a stricter responsibility for young men under a law with punishment for having sex with a virgin without a clear and serious intention. The law would include a moral reprimand and a financial penalty that is no small fine and will become future debt if the young man can't pay at the time for using innocent girls. Also, it could be helpful to give public censure to these men as special moral message. We can't allow young men the freedom of having sex in any circumstances without concern for innocence of our young women, who need to be psychologically healthy to give birth and raise a healthy new population of individuals and intellectuals.

We can't be rational and prudent and allow men of all ages to use the services of prostitutes or single women, who are trying to live their lives by rules and honor, without disturbing the community's structure. We can't blame women who have sex with men and at the same time condone the same action by men if we want universal happiness and equal rights for all humanity. If the male population stopped suffering financially after entering into a marriage contract and women stopped being solely responsible for raising and watching kids, maybe marriage would be a more advanced institution and become a salvation for the sexual needs of humans.

If we are not committing adultery, or having sex without the intention of marriage, or taking away a person's sexual partner as mentioned in religious scripts, we might reduce difficulties in all areas of realization of our instinct of survival and reproduction, and continue to create a healthy new generation.

The next most broken commandment is the directive not to steal, which has been analyzed in different sources as strictly robbery. The novel *Les Miserables* by Victor Hugo described serious contradictions when a hungry man stole a piece of bread and was punished by serving time in a prison and then gave into the temptation of stealing again when severe circumstances pushed him. Fortunately, the victim of the second robbery in the life of the hero was a priest who allowed him to take the stolen items as a gift, eliminating our hero's liability for the breach of this commandment. Then the hero of this unique novel is transformed into an honest man with many good qualities, respect for the basic values of society, and more.

We can conclude that is only a unique story that is fiction and that nothing like this can happen in real life. However, the idea of this novel doesn't reject the return to the true course of creation and honest work after someone has suffered a penalty and received a secondary chance in life to return to the previous system of values, which was corrupted because of extreme circumstances in life.

Society has tolerated many sources of wealth of people who at any point in their lives returned to higher standards of existence and implemented this immortal commandment, as we can see today.

Critical assumptions of sins and events that happen with different members of our community often get mixed up with exaggerations, distortions, and conclusions that are far from reality because it is convenient to see things that way. However, if everyone asked him—or herself or others how it is right and how it indisputably coordinates with the classical principle of "don't make false statements about your fellow," all of mankind would be less of a problem.

Throughout the centuries one group of people has attacked and occupied the lands of others groups of people in acts of war. Unfortunately, this is the only method that exists at the present time. There would be undeniably less ugly forms of force and war if it was possible to bring into existence one set of laws for the entire planet without prioritizing any group of people in the solution for this very difficult question.

The democratic approach is the only way for all people, who are equal and dedicated to their own communities, and the most realistic form of realization of this task and happiness for the entire human race. Only real contributions for progress and prosperity of humanity can be a priority in the criteria of a solution to these questions about the lands of people. In other aspects of this principle, concordant to the laws of each specific country, we must defend the interest and right of every person to own a house or rent a home.

CHAPTER IV

DETERMINATION OF NEGATIVE WAYS OF THINKING

Some books, like *Cognitive Therapy* by Judith S. Beck (1995), wonderfully describe the basic forms of negative thinking, and the examples in this chapter are devised on the basis of examples from this source, which are as follows:

1. All-or-nothing (also called black-and-white, polarized, or dichotomous thinking) *Example:* "If all my colleagues were not pleased with my work, then nothing proves my work is valuable."

2. Catastrophization (also called fortune-telling) *Example:* "I'll be so miserable I won't be able to make a speech at all."

3. Disqualifying or discounting the positive
   Example: "I wrote this composition excellently, but that doesn't mean I'm talented. I just got lucky."

4. Emotional reasoning
   Example: "I know I do a lot of things perfectly, but I still feel like I'm defective."

5. Labeling *Examples:* "I'm so stupid" and "He's not strong."

6. Magnification/minimization
    Examples: "She only gave me a nod. That proves my behavior is unacceptable" and "I got all As, but it doesn't mean I'm smart."

7. Mental filter (also called selective abstraction)
    Example: "My boss complimented my work, but because I made one mistake, it means I'm doing a lousy job."

8. Mind reader
    Example: "He's thinking I am incompetent in my job, so he gives me advice."

9. Overgeneralization *Example:* "I commonly lose things, which means I don't have what it takes to make friends."

10. Personalization *Example:* "The coworker doesn't greet me because I'm sneezing today."

11. "Should" and "must" statements (also called imperatives): *Example:* "It's terrible that I didn't spell one word correctly in my report. I should be always accurate in my work."

12. Tunnel vision:
    Example: "My son's teacher doesn't give him good grades. He's an unfair, cruel, and incompetent teacher."

This list and assembled examples of negative ways of thinking is basic, and I would like to explore these examples in greater detail with illustrations. These kinds of thoughts could support depressive symptoms and cause dysfunctional behavior that affects our lives and the lives of other people. Sometimes they sound almost logical and normal, but in reality they are reflected, distorted, and dysfunctional conclusions and behavior.

To better demonstrate each form of negative thinking, I have isolated them and in some cases have matched them with illustrations.

The following examples are based on the definitions of Judith S. Beck (1995) and are followed by examples of corresponding thoughts and my explanation of the type of negative thinking.

ALL-OR-NOTHING

Definition: You see a situation in only two opposite categories.

Example: "If all my colleagues were not pleased with my work, then nothing proves my work is valuable."

The person who experiences this category of thinking comes to narrow conclusions and dysfunctional actions, missing much of what is positive in the gray intermediate areas. This personality, on one side, never feels satisfied if things in life do not occur accurately to match the high standards and perfect ideals that are desired and predicted by this person. On the other side, this person doesn't allow any error, inaccuracy, or any other lesser result that differs from his or her desired schema, and he or she is crushed by poor fallouts and misses recognizing other smaller possibilities, choices, and opportunities.

This sketch is an example of all-or-nothing negative thinking.

Instead, this incorrect negative thinking makes it possible to use a positive realistic conclusion to modify it: "Even if all colleagues were not pleased with my work, it remains valuable in larger its parts."

The possible positive reality-based interpretations could considerably help a person who demonstrates a tendency toward all-or-nothing thinking to modify the distortions and replace them with more precise corrections that reflect reality-based positive interpretations in the different situations. It can also help for the other distorted negative types of the thinking discussed in this chapter.

Catastrophization

Definition: You predict the future in an exaggerated, negative form.

Example: "I'll be so miserable I won't be able to make a speech at all."

The person who experiences this type of negative thinking can't distinguish any positive aspects in the future. Catastrophic phenomena are the only imaginary results and options.

This person is completely missing other solutions and possibilities that will lower or even liquidate problems in the future. Instead of concentrating on solutions to problems and reducing the probability of misfortunes, the person is anxious and worries because of fear and poor ideas that possibly exist only in his or her mind.

This sketch is an example of the catastrophization type of negative thinking.

A positive interpretation of this example could be as follows: "I will be prepared thoroughly for my speech tomorrow, I will do my best, and I will look and speak in my finest manner."

DISQUALIFYING THE POSITIVE

Definition: You groundlessly tell yourselves that positive situations, your qualities, and your merits are ineffective.

Example: "I wrote this composition excellent, but that doesn't mean I'm talented. I just got lucky."

A person who is inclined to and experienced in this form of dysfunctional thinking makes self-defeating statements that frequently lead to minimizing or even failing to recognize his or her own good qualities. He or she believes that anything he or she does doesn't count, denying his or her qualifications. This person concludes that nothing he or she made has value, that only other people pose the truthful qualities, and that only their opinions and experiences are important and meaningful. The person with this kind of distortion completely denies his or her own significance and capability for correct actions and competence in anything. Everything related to this person doesn't matter and isn't considerable or important. This person sees any situation as negative, despite opposite and obvious circumstances or evidence.

This sketch is an example of the disqualifying the positive type of negative thinking.

Instead of this incorrect conclusion, the thought should be used a different way: "I wrote this composition excellently because I worked hard. I am capable and good at what I do. If I continue to be zealous, I will achieve the same success again."

EMOTIONAL REASONING

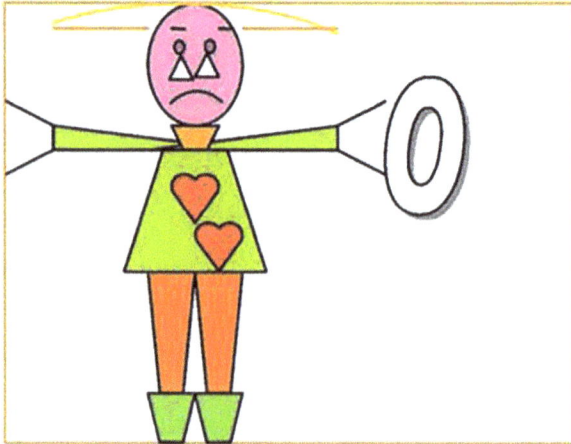

Definition: You think this must be truth, disregarding the obvious facts because you "feel" so.

Example: "I know I do a lot of things perfectly, but I still feel like I'm defective."

This person's emotional state defines how he or she relates to different facts, no matter what the evidences is. In this case, it appears that the absence of satisfaction in anything this person does dominates in his or her way of thinking. This form of distortion supports only negative interpretations, excluding obvious facts and proof of the reverse, because the person has strong feelings that are opposite to reality. In this case, unreasonable emotions and distorted negative thinking are sometimes based on a previous negative view of self, which can never be good because of past errors, failures, sins, and oversights. These failings don't allow expiating; therefore the person cannot confirm present progress in any part or area of his or her life and will never believe approval or gratification in anything. This person uses negative selfappraisal about his or her own behavior, merits, and situations, and negative interpretations of real-life circumstances.

This sketch is an example of the emotional reasoning type of negative thinking.

Instead, this incorrect conclusion could be modified in the following way: "I know I do a lot of things perfectly. It is fine for me to admit that and be proud of the fact that it is the result of my hard and persistent work."

LABELING

Definition: You place an inclusive label on yourself and others that has no evidence or basis in proof and is without reasons special to that and doesn't allow for other options that might be more plausible and lead to a less fixed conclusion.

Examples: "I'm so stupid" and "He's not strong."

Labeling is assigning a precise and rigid negative definition for each and every person without any opportunity to amend the standard, absolute perception. This prevents any chance of replacing the label with a proven converse declaration or obvious proof of the opposite because of the inertia in the thought process or because it is convenient to believe it this way.

When it occurs, it becomes more difficult to reason and think differently, which is more inconvenient than keeping a low rating of oneself or others. Nothing seems more reliable or worth it versus pursuing the favorite canons, rules, and customs that reflect regular and ordinary opinions or points of view. It is easier to think about standard categories than it is to take a flexible and less rigid individual approach to different circumstances, or to accept new proven qualities that the person failed to recognize for a long time and persistently had not noticed in spite of everything. This kind of thinking is customized mostly in present society for different reasons, largely for expediency in declining other choices of priority instead of the old one everybody is used to, even when all evidences point to the opposite.

These sketches are examples of labeling.

Instead of this approach, it is appropriate to replace the labeling thoughts with interpretations:

"I could do better than that" and "He could be stronger in other situations."

Magnification/minimization

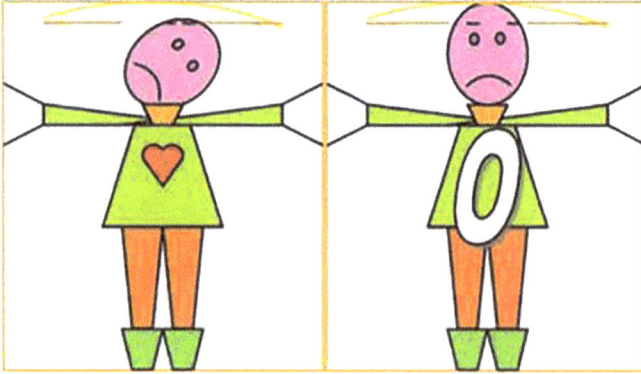

Definition: When you estimate yourself, another person, or a situation, you irrationally exaggerate the negative and/or diminish the positive.

Examples: "She only gave me a nod. That proves how inadequate I am" and "I got all As, but it doesn't mean I'm smart."

The person who has magnification/minimization dysfunctional thinking extremely exaggerates anything that happened in a negative way, drawing extreme conclusions from minimal signs or reasons to think this way. This person denies any other benign or positive explanations and lacks the vision of the real picture or other feasible explanations. This leads to an exaggeration of poor sides and understating good sides, without any essential reason or verification for a similar conclusion. Therefore this person misses the positive aspects and events that are happening in the favorable field of sight and representing the more iridescent picture of life. Unrealistic and negative interpretations incline a person to be suspicious and to have no objectivity in judgment, which causes dysfunctional and incorrect thinking and behavior. This person minimizes all good qualities, options, and opportunities because he or she concentrates on only negative explanations, conclusions, and possibilities that have little chance of happening.

These sketches are examples of the magnification/minimization type of negative thinking.

Realistic proposals could be correct in this more appropriate way:

She gave me only a nod and didn't talk to me because she rushed to go to important meeting. I got all "A's", it means I have excellent level of education.

MENTAL FILTER

Definition: You notice only one negative component or feature instead of enveloping the entire picture as a whole.

Example: "My boss complimented my work, but because I made one mistake, it means I'm doing a lousy job."

With this form of negative thinking, a person perceives any small error, inaccuracy, or deficiency as a complete tragedy and having appeared with the unusual clearness of only negative results, which are void of other capacities and merits. This kind of negative thinking has a tendency to concentrate on one negative detail with very small and unremarkable significance; this detail appears for this person as a calamity and is pictured as a negative effect that discards other valuable qualities and huge parts of developments.

Inability to recognize positive in anything leads to the observation of minimal, insignificant faults, the smallest and unessential deficiencies, nonobjective and untruthful estimations of reality, and negation of the value of others that neglects huge valuable parts in everything. This irrational dysfunctional thinking will deny the excellent half of truth if the truth is not perfect and contains any small mistake or insufficiency. Nothing is complete or good enough if this doesn't comply with the ideal schema. It can't be final and acceptable if it has some flaws and if it is not brought to perfection. It erases an entire piece of great work without any doubts. This thinking complicates any development and underestimates the achievements of any person; it also prevents the progress of beginners if they think their reality isn't absolutely perfect.

More realistically this sentence might be assumed as follow:

My work was noticed and highly estimated by my boss despite a small and insignificant mistake.

MIND READER

Definition: You think that you distinguish exactly what is in other people's minds, excluding possible and more realistic explanations.

Example: "He's thinking I am incompetent in my job, so he gives me advice."

This thinking isn't effective or functional because the person who has been experiencing this form of conclusion believes that he or she knows exactly and definitely how others are thinking, without considering different, more realistic, and mostly benign explanations and interpretations of other people's intentions. This person operates predictions that indicate his or her point of view, which is different from reality. This individual suggests only negative and unrealistic fantasies of how other must think.

This personality builds his or her own hypothesized theories based on imaginable negative conclusions and absolute ideas that are singularly truthful because he or she believes in them. What he perceives, hears, and sees that nearly reflect his subjective past experiences, or even other people's experiences, or obstacles is far from the real present situation and distant from truth, or they are facts that have been described somewhere in different doubtable sources. This person doesn't allow him—or herself to distinguish other options or suggest more realistic interpretations.

As an alternative, we can change this negative thought to the following: "He gives me advice with good intentions. I am ready to listen to him in spite of my other vision of the situation and think about it."

OVERGENERALIZATION

Definition: You make a general unconstructive conclusion in all instances on the basis of one or several doubtable facts that are distant from the existing situation.

Example: "I commonly lose things, which means I don't have what it takes to make friends." The person who experiences this type of negative thinking lacks particular and undoubted facts, which often leads to overgeneralization and errors in conclusions; this person has a tendency to overestimate his or her poor information and jump to the wrong conclusions and actions. He or she often accepts imaginable perception as reality, even if only one fact has been proven by the imaginable situation. This person can draw in his or her mind lacking facts without evident proof, precise data, real experiences, or obstacles. The mistake comes from underlying beliefs that he or she is always correct and fair and has absolutely perfect personality. This person believes that only he or she has great, undoubted experiences in everything.

He or she doesn't accept real evidence or new correct data in a current situation, especially if this existing situation gives the illusion of an identical situation from the past; then it is very difficult for this person to tell the difference.

The incorrect thought (sentence) can be replaced with a more realistic explanation: "I don't have friends for other reasons, but not because I am losing things, which is a result of my distraction and poor attention."

PERSONALIZATION

Definition: You believe that others behave negatively in relation to you because of some reason in you, without allowing for more conceivable explanations for their behavior.

Example: "My coworker doesn't greet me because I am sneezing today."

All negative events that occur with a person who is experiencing this type of thinking have been inverted to him. Because of his or her fault, error, shortage, and inaccuracy, this person is responsible for everything, and he or she needs to be blamed for it.

Other explanations, even those more genuine and accurate, slip from this person's attention. All obstacles that took place in other circumstances are not taken into consideration and are eliminated from the equation as countable, reasonable, or valuable. Even disasters or accidents that occur in different places are related to this person by invisible threads that somehow lead to him or her. Therefore this personality has been influenced mystically and unfortunately, proceeding along an unlucky path through his or her imagined fault. This individual imagines that he or she causes accidents and catastrophes.

This person believes that he or she attracts only negative events, without confirmation or evidence. Everything horrific is magically connected to this person, and as a consequence of this distortion in his or her thinking, he or she experiences various problems.

This person is experienced in dysfunctional thinking that everything negative is related to him or her, without consideration of other more realistic explanations for different disturbances in his or her feelings, behavior, and condition. This person without any evidence has placed himself in center of everything dreadful that happens around him or her, and even beyond.

This sketch is an example of personalization.

Instead of this conclusion, it is possible to come to a more realistic and possible replacement: "My coworker didn't greet me because evidently she didn't see me."

"SHOULD" AND "MUST"

Definition: You have precise, flat ideas of how you and others must act, and you overrate how appalling it is that hopes are not met and everything goes otherwise.

Example: "It's terrible that I didn't spell one word correctly in my report. I should always be accurate in my work."

The person with this type of negative thinking is convinced that even a small inaccuracy in reality leads to worse consequences, and that it's necessary to perform everything precisely and accurately in the way it is supposed to be, or requested to be, in exactly designed schemas. Nothing disrupts or strays from the rules, and everyone must proceed in a definite way, by order. Everything needs to be done exactly and precisely without the smallest deviation or change or ignorance of established rules.

This person constantly pushes from the inside and loses peace and sleep if something is not completed exactly according to a precise schema or is done wrong in any way, in spite of the big price that will need to be paid or the great effort that will need to be put in, and despite facts of new requirements and changes of reality. The same rules apply to other people. If anybody slips from precise schema, it's so wrong, unacceptable, and terrible that he or she will need to be judged, shamed, and condemned.

This sketch is an example of "should" and "must" negative thinking.

Precise thinking is more logical and positive with the following conclusion: "Nobody paid attention to my small mistake in the report, and generally most people loved it."

TUNNEL VISION

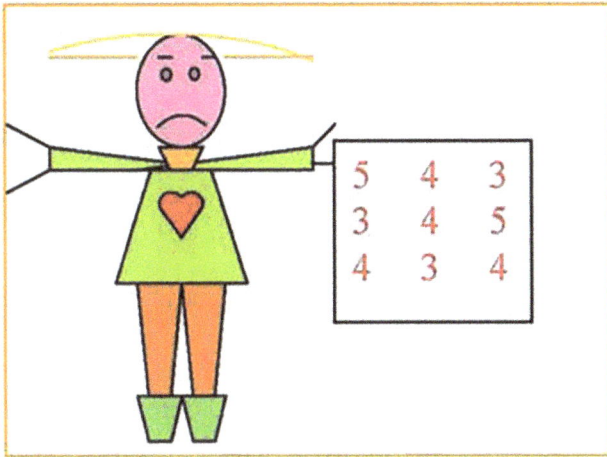

Definition: You only observe the negative sides in any situation.

Example: "My son's teacher doesn't give him good grades. He's an unfair, cruel, and incompetent teacher."

In this sort of thinking, the person sees only unrealistically negative and dark sides of situations that are incommensurable with the reality. He or she fails to pay attention to positive facts and events in life. This person doesn't notice how much he or she has done, superior qualities of other people that can be encouraging, or good options or events that have happened in reality. Only negative occurrences have priority in his or her sight. This person misses all positive sides and pays attention only to pessimistic facts or signs, which plead, reduce, or even erase the entire prehistory or complexity of good phenomena. He or she declines all previous good experiences and denies multiple positive events. This person sees only the rotten fruit in a beautiful garden and notices tiny cobwebs in crystal-clear pond. He pays attention specifically to negative obstacles and "fishes out" only deficiencies, shortages, and mistakes despite other large fine qualities and features.

This sketch is an example of tunnel vision.

It is correct to suggest a more positive conclusion that corresponds to reality: "Despite the efforts of the teacher, my son earns bad grades with good grades sometimes. Maybe my son needs the help of a tutor."

CHAPTER V

DISCUSSION OF OTHER TYPES OF NEGATIVE THINKING

BLAMING

B laming is another form of invalid conceptualization that can be manifested in blaming oneself or other people. In the case of unreasonable blaming, when a person blames others unjustifiably, this is an expressed projection of his or her own failures at other people's expense. For some reason, it seems very convenient to this person to accuse the people surrounding him or her and to put others in the center of his or her own misfortunes and mistakes rather than concede his or her role in the emergent trouble or take action to solve it.

Instead of this, it is easier to implicate other people and through blame force someone to resolve situation. In the press, books, and television shows, we observe many clear examples of blame toward different groups of people or a specific person when shocking or even tragic events happen, including even exceptionally critical facts. Obviously, society's leaders have taken global blame for many things for which they were not responsible—things that were caused by poor analysis of the social structure, financial predispositions, the corruption of moral abutments, or other reasons.

In a sense, children can be the object of attack and blame by their parents for things they did not cause or did not have the intention to do. Beyond this, guilt remains a heavy burden and affects their future fate, which leads to the loss of their ability to build healthy relationships without superfluous blaming of others. In addition, relationships of couples can include the blaming of each other, and this creates an unhealthy affiliation between partners.

Self-blame is a very frequent conception of negative thinking. In this case, a person unreasonably blames him—or herself for all misfortunes that happen around him or her. Because one or even more people erroneously blame this person, it seems true, despite the evidence that does not support it; the person involved in this trouble is not the only one involved in this adverse reality. The individual, in this instance, is taking excessive responsibility for his or her surrounding situation, exaggerating his or her own unfortunate role in a way that reflects a negative way of thinking—self-blaming.

PERFECTIONISM

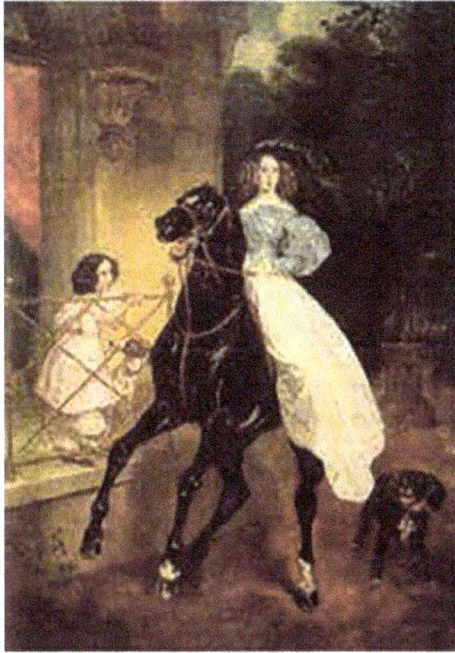

Perfectionism occurs often as a negative perception of reality that unrealistically exaggerates one's own or other people's harmonious abilities to achieve certain exceptional qualities and merits, or to make special things and create something desirable, all without objectivity and substantiation to a person's prerequisites and predispositions. Kozma Prutkov wrote that a person who creates himself as ideal or an idol is leaving only a stone monument for himself that excludes his normal human existence. There is also a quotation for this aphorism in religious scripts: "…And you shall not erect for yourselves a pillar…"

In fact, modesty is not only part of the beautiful human personality and a decoration of human soul, but it also helps us live uncomplicated human lives. Instead of concentrating on efforts and attempts, a perfectionist is focused only on the results and achievements that make an immense difference with people who keep soul-searching, exercising noble creativity, or challenging themselves to improve their and other people's lives, as well as the things around them.

The perfectionist is never happy by any results if they are far from the planned accomplishment and are without precise perfection or are not very close to desirable quality. This person has a purpose to exclusively achieve the ideal; he or she forces and wastes him—or herself and others in making unreasonable sacrifices and superhuman efforts that negatively affect their lives. Therefore, the changes are produced without taking into account actual conditions, circumstances, and reasonable limitations. The perfectionist can't accept his or her own or other people's insolvency to live according to high standards and can't allow smaller levels in any achievement without comprehension and revision of the obstacles that prevent other people or him—or herself to get the advanced quality of living.

DOUBLE STANDARD

A double standard refers to a misconception in thinking that could be applied to yourself or others. It means a person places very high standards on him—or herself and allows others to follow lesser standards and step back from demands that the person requires him—or herself to handle. Or, on the other hand, a person incorporates very strict superfluous requirements and rigid rules on others and always makes an exception for him—or herself, permitting and justifying without reasons special for that occasion.

When the person asks him—or herself for a lot more than others, he or she is preoccupied with the first version of double standard negative thinking in which this person can't forgive him—or herself for mistakes and at the same time assumes others have no mistakes or deficiencies. Furthermore, this person severely tortures him—or herself for inadvertence, is hard on him—or herself, pardons others' indiscretions, and is forgiving and kind for others' shortages. He renders praise and honor to the merits and achievements of others and never appreciates his or her own achievements and accomplishments. This person torments him—or herself for behavior that is considered permissible for others and treats him—or herself less fairly than others in identical situations.

Alternatively, consider another version of the double standard negative assumption when a person sets strict rules for others and makes an exception for him—or herself and gives him—or herself permission for much more than other people. Nobody is allowed to violate or tolerate disruption or disobedience of the rules constructed by this person, but at the same time this does not apply to this person; the exception is only for him or her. Other people must think about this person; satisfy his or her needs; surround and embrace him or her with extremely high attention; and observe distance, rules, and installations in any situation—all without disrupting the rules and installation of this personality.

It appears that those rules are not strictly connected to this person because he or she always has excuses and obstacles that allow him or her to avoid many restrictions, boundaries, and limitations. The fact is that this person is convinced by justifications and formulated good explanations that others need to follow many rules for his or her convenience and why he or she doesn't don't have to (also for his or her sake).

THINKING OF REJECTION

Thoughts of rejection demonstrate other distorted conceptions in a person's thinking process and represent unpleasant feelings and suffering about being rejected by others. Frequently, these thoughts stop a person from undertaking attempts to improve his or her life. Thoughts about rejection suppress a young man from showing affection to a desirable woman or prevent a woman from making a decision to begin a relationship with the person she loves.

Furthermore, many developments can't even start because self-doubts and fear of rejection in creative work avert the opening of new roads for progress. Once rejected, the person doesn't hurry to make another attempt and instead selects a reliable way of life, one without troubles. He or she is afraid of giving one more chance to start or have a new opportunity. The person chooses a plain and safe life without new challenges and follows boring schemas, which often leads to mental disorder.

Instead of analysis and an objective approach to the facts that led to the rejected feelings and ideas, this person experiences self-doubts and regrets about failure, which are expressed through underestimation of the factors, which leads to disappointment and curtails further useful and valuable efforts toward change, progress, and success. The person avoids beginning something unknowing, risk-taking, responsibility, or challenge, and he or she doesn't allow assumption about other more positive possible explanations for failure. Under the effect of his or her feelings of rejection, this person can't suggest that he or she was rejected for other reasons like obstacles that are not involved with him. Neither can the person justify a failure that might contain temporarily limitations that can be overcome with work and zeal. Instead, this person is crushed by rejection and unreasonably becomes disappointed, depressed, anxious, and angry with others and him—or herself.

EXPECTING APPROVAL

Everyone waits for the recognition and support in their endeavors of others, under the influence of uncertainty that what he or she is doing is the right thing. In the absence of that support, a person cannot synthesize prior knowledge like people who don't have any experience. It happens when someone arrives to live in a new place or acquires a new job or considers starting fresh from scratch. To some extent, this person can't imagine that his or her qualities remain similar and persists in viewing his or her achievements or accomplishments as untouchable and deniable in spite of a new environment or community. Instead, this person can't recognize that his or her existence doesn't need approval at all times in his or her life and that he or she needs to trust previous experiences from the best part of his or her life that support confidence and self-assurance as approval, without conformation of judgment of other people.

Such people become accustomed to constantly seeking endorsement and sympathy in other people. They prefer to listen to the council of others and don't trust their own sensations and information they accumulated in the past. They can't admit their own dignity and significance, which could give them control over their lives and success.

According to famous writer A. P. Chekhov, everyone has equality as a human being, despite differences in circumstances and merits. When a young person looks to the future with hope of recognition and affirmation of his or her merit, as well as affirmation of the correctness of his or her actions toward other people, he or she is full of confidence in the dream of finding a worthy position in society. This young person is strong enough and equal for the tasks. If this personality gets a negative acknowledgement of his or her actions once or a few times, the person becomes pessimistic toward his or her own abilities. This is sometimes true and is occasionally the result of a confluence of adverse circumstances.

Unfortunately, we often do not receive support and recognition from people who are occupied by their own problems and challenges, and waiting for their sympathy is a waste of time. In these cases, faith in one's own luck and abilities along with challenging one's own life in sync with others' will help a person establish balance in his or her life simultaneously in society.

However, it is still doubtable and depressing from time to time. Only consciousness of many efforts and missing possibilities will synchronously balance one's own approval with the conformation of others. One must also consider the following: If our achievements do not violate the peace and confidence of other people, if this is a new path to success of many people and adds something positive forgotten from the past, then it can be well understood by other people, and quite rightly, that we tend to have the support of those who are close to us (family, friends, coworkers, and many others) without hesitation.

MISTAKEN IDENTITY

This way of dysfunctional thinking reflects a much understated estimation and even negation of one's own personality, which is not worthy in the base of the realization of mistakes of the past. In this case, a person considers him—or herself awful and unworthy and believes he or she cannot be equal to other dignified and noble people. This person cannot forgive his or her past errors, which diminishes all his or her achievements and doesn't give the person the right to respect him—or herself. In this kind of distorted thinking, the person can't distinguish the fact that making mistakes is in human nature, which he or she can or can't correct. This doesn't make him or her a bad person; it determines the essence of a human being. This person should learn to forgive him—or herself, continue to look forward, attempt to correct past mistakes, and not repeat them. However, if the person makes the same mistakes over and over again, he or she can forgive him—or herself and define the nature of origin of these errors without hatred for him—or herself. We are designed to make mistakes and feel pain for them.

Thereby, we learn to accept bitter experiences and correct them only without thinking of ourselves as a "mistaken identity" and self-hate, which includes thinking about one's own "faults" or "defective" personality. We can make mistakes for many reasons, and this includes how we apply our basic belief system, which we already mentioned in previous chapters. Our belief system reflects exceptional concepts; nobody can observe these basic human values 100 percent of the time or be ideal. Just as we have called ourselves "mistaken identities," in the same way we can apply the name "false identity" for other people. Instead of pointing and noticing other people's errors, we should focus on other good qualities and display humanism and compassion. We should learn to pardon other people and their errors just as we pardon ourselves and our mistakes.

Egocentric Thinking

Egocentric negative misconceptions in thinking reflect a person's desire and confidence that other people think as he does, without indulgent facts others view differently, and don't follow the perfect schemas that are packed this person's mind. But this person follows them and expects other people do the same. As a result of this error, this person experiences severely indescribable disappointments and starts to blame others because they don't obey rules, which the ego-centric person has strictly been following; he or she believes other interpretations cannot exist.

We share basic beliefs, but as mentioned in previous chapters, people disobey them in order to carry out principles of survival or to satisfy their own needs, which has led to confusion and vagueness among people. In particular, it generates an egocentric way of the thinking—for example, the mindset of the terrorist group that led the attack on September 11, 2001, destroying thousands of innocent lives in the World Trade Center tragedy, as well as other tragic events in different parts of the world.

In those confusing circumstances, the only way to reduce egocentric thinking is to accept the facts that were pointed out above (why not all people follow the rules), to understand how to accept differences in thinking, beliefs, and behavior in different groups of people, and to manifest respect for other points of view.

Egocentric negative thinking does not consider and does not pursue validation of other people's feelings and beliefs if they differ from the personal ideal schema of the egocentric individual, who takes charge in deciding how things have to be without realistically considering the differences between people's feelings, thoughts, and behavior. It exists in two negative ways: first, when the egocentric person is hurting people around him or her, and second, when as a result, those people's disapproval and resistance bring troubles for the egocentric person also.

EMPTY OF SELF

Emptiness is a kind of emotional reasoning that reflects in a person's negative thinking that he or she is empty and void because he or she has been feeling this way. This person has declined any evidence that he or she is valuable, interesting, or gifted or has abilities or something meant for him or her, because he or she feels numbness— no regret, no pain, no love, no worries—and mostly void. Instead, this person concentrates on his or her preferences and takes chances in challenging his or her life. He or she finds it more optimal to maintain resistance to involvement with others or previous enjoyable activities, and more deeply departs to the sensations of emptiness and insipidness.

This person doesn't have any motive or drive to take the risk of new experiences and sensations. Furthermore, he or she follows distorted schemas in thinking and patterns of behavior that deceive this person and amplify his or her feeling of devastation. This person also experiences fear of rejection and disappointment. He or she can't find anything more interesting because of inertia, which comes from past and continues to affect this person's life. The best solution for this kind of negative thinking is visualizations, predictions, and imaginations of positive vivid pictures of pleasure and enjoyable events until the person returns to normal life activities and normal reality-based thinking and has a restored sense of joy in life.

In the famous short novel *White Nights*, F. Dostoyevsky vividly shows the trick a melancholy person uses to avoid sincere devastation in dreams and iridescent ideas while trying to overcome his thinking of self-emptiness. The person questions himself about what is making sense in his life. This means this person might have been experiencing empty of self negative thinking. The best answer might sound like this: it means finding a sense of joy in small charms and pleasures and living life for life itself!

FAKERY

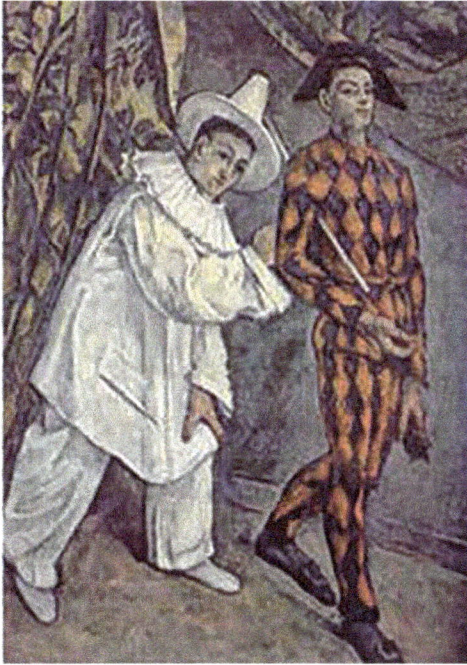

Fakery is the most contradictive negative thinking, and it is often mixed with pretending, deception, and lies that really affect the life of a community. Wearing masks, performing different roles, and playing games—in other words, simulation—represent the socializa-tion of most people, which must be distinguished from false and deceptive hypocrisy that disrupts the balance of standards in society. Social bonds between people frequently include games and wearing masks for convenience and acceptable, polite contact, which indi-cates the healthy covering of truth, which is not so important for the preservation of the peace and rest of society. If we don't tell a person that he or she looks unwell, it doesn't mean we are not truthful; we are using common sense and friendly relations as part of etiquette and good manners.

In the other case, we don't tell truth and we lie, which is aimed at undermining the interests of a person in any manner. Then we can speak about the hypocrisy, the lie, and the unhealthy motives. This especially vividly comes out when we consciously disrupt our basic values or unreasonably break them and don't implement bestjudgment in applying our system of values; we become liars, in the true sense of this word. Exercising fakery is the main part of social skills, and the way we choose our masks defines our individual preferences.

As we mentioned earlier, the simulation of emotions and playing roles is part of good manners. And how we select one or another form of fakery according to social status and the adequate social situation determines a good adaptation and normal behavior accepted in society, and distinguishes our individuality from other people.

EXPECTING OF PUNISHMENT

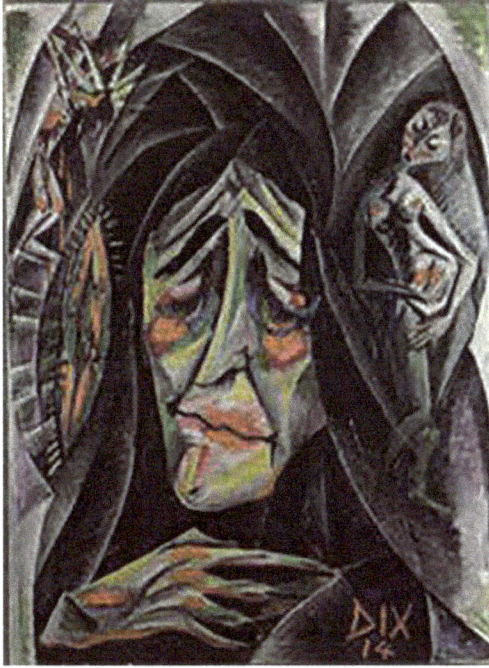

The expectation of punishment as a negative form of thinking originates from the belief that we deserve punishment for something we did wrong or didn't do right. However, many things and events occur without reasons, are not connected with the punishment, and are called bad luck according to disharmony in the world, which was discussed in previous chapters. Sometimes we bear reasonably punishment by the law of the people; sometimes we don't. If we have acknowledged our disharmony by following the basic system of values that produces experience with and expectations of punishment, tremendous guilt, and anxiety, we understand that nothing comes without our intrinsic justice, which can be controlled. We can realize that in our reason, nothing occurs without beliefs, which are temporarily hidden in the corners of our unconsciousness. But unexpectedly they can become obvious and acknowledged by our minds. So it is necessary to control our beliefs and, as a result of that, control our thoughts and emotions.

We can analyze why we have distorted the system of values we violated, which reflects distorted interpretations of the true values; incorrect judgment; and unawareness that our distortions have been accommodated because we were under the pressure of survival. (As discussed in previous chapters, we can afford to follow only 60-70 percent of our beliefs in order to survive and meet our own needs). We can also face the same results in view of errors and inadequate interpretations of the main system of values by other people (i.e., become victims of the bad judgment and distortion of other people's thinking and their wrong interpretation of the basic belief system). Fear of punishment depends to a large degree on conflict in our own belief system and can be controlled by revision and change in our dysfunctional thinking and behavior (which is based on an irrational belief system) to establish reason in our own and other people's obedience to basic values.

THINKING OF REVENGE

Thinking of revenge is not a rare type of negative thinking, but it disturbs our peace and produces unwanted actions and circumstances. If the Count of Monte Cristo—the hero of a famous novel by French writer Alexander Dumas—had concentrated on his efforts to do more useful things instead of experiencing guilt for the punishment of innocent people as a result of his revenge, he could have been a happier person. This could also have happened if he had found the strength to forgive his enemies and forget the tremendous humiliation that affected his life. It could also have been fortunate for him to concentrate on discovering the incredible treasure and building a new life. But instead he preferred revenge and became the dark force that punished everything related to his unfortunate experiences.

Some religious sources offer to forgive and forget any offense and look for justice by law, which contradicts others who look for revenge. What we can get with revenge, instead, is injustice and the placement of ourselves and others in a very complicated situation. If we talk about small things that make us look to revenge, we could be much happier if we forgave or told others in a controlled way how bad it was, without thinking and feeling all the complex emotions that could destroy our lives and health. Revenge supports loneliness, mistrust of others, and wishes to always get your own back. Making things bad for others as revenge can't make you happier, and it puts you in the position of being as bad of a person as the people who did badly to you. You become a bad person who you hate, and this could make things worse for you, increase feelings of desperation, put you in a position of being a bad person, and increase ugliness, injustice, and unhappiness in the world...

ANGER

Angry thoughts accompany us when we are sure that things need to be a certain way, when we expect different outcomes, when we lose something very dear to our hearts, when we feel betrayed and deceived, or when we can't explain why things and people are so irritable to us. Angry thoughts can be acknowledged or unconscious. We might display angry outbursts or keep our anger to ourselves and divert it toward ourselves, or we might turn this anger against others in an indirect way that is called by some sources passive-aggressive behavior.

This kind of negative thinking hurts us and others, and it is very important how we deal with this anger. As mentioned earlier, angry thinking can be controlled in several ways: replacing, reforming, decatastrophizing, diminishing the meaning of the offense, forgiving oneself and others, looking at the roots of this thinking and feeling, using positive interpretations of other people's intentions and mistakes, comparing with one's own motivation, and giving second or more chances. We also might divert from anger toward our chores and procreative activities by giving space, pausing in unpleasant interactions, and always being reasonable and adequate.

Social Comparison

Social comparison is essential for developing appropriate social skills; however, it could be very wrong when someone uses it in a negative and irrational way. Social comparison is a very relative form of our place in society that is also defined by our options, limitations, possibilities, roots, etc. This is a basic implication of our social lives and a great motivation in life to be like other people or even better. If suddenly we decide that others are better in some way, this can produce very unpleasant and uncomfortable feelings that "drive some people crazy." This reaction is called envy, which reflects an unhealthy form of social comparison (that is also controlled by the basic belief system).

If we feel excessive guilt for exercising social comparison, we could be irrational also. Constant comparison with others in healthy ways helps a person adapt to a new environment, a new society, or other new circumstances. Every person needs to be like everybody else; this defines his or her mental sanity and appropriate behavior. We are required to wear some masks and display suitable behavior that society decides is appropriate.

People play different roles that fit the present situation and are acceptable in society. Role-playing and modeling are basic techniques for developing appropriate social and communication skills. An individual who uses social comparison to define his or her individuality by choosing specific available masks or a combination of different masks and styles of behavior is developing his or her own pattern of thinking and behavior that society approves of as suitable at the present time.

If the person has a poor ability to copy other people (as a result of isolation, lack of education, no appropriate role model, family dysfunctions, or severe mental disturbances, genetically or biologically), he or she looks like an inappropriate person. Some people who use their basic belief system (basic values) appropriately don't seem to be wearing masks because their behavior becomes natural and pleasant and reflects their unconscious pattern of thinking and behavior. People who are just copying those people, without the implication of their basic belief system (basic values), often don't seem natural; they look like people wearing masks, playing different roles like bad or good actors.

Guilt

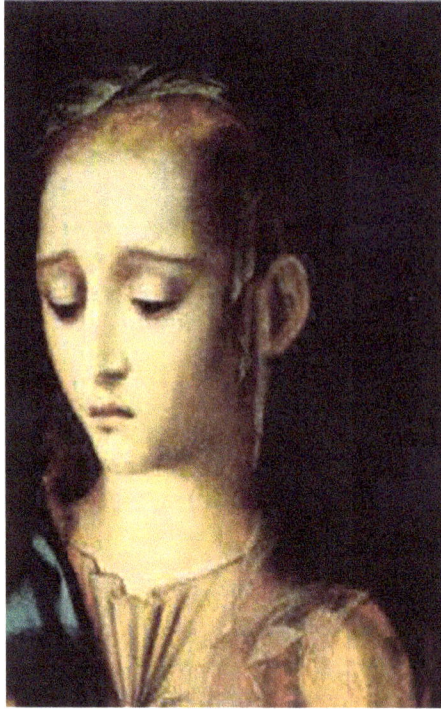

Guilt also results in a different kind of negative thinking. Guilt depends on appropriate use of our basic belief system and reflects different distortions in it and our interpretations of it, as well as conflicts between our beliefs and our needs. If we don't learn how to bargain and deal with our belief system, we will experience constant feelings of guilt.

We need to use positive reality-based interpretations, compromise reasonably, be flexible, deviate from rigid schemas, and implicate real-life situations to our basic belief system without corruption and inertia back to it. Different kinds of art, books, movies, and television shows help us to choose the right model (or the right interpretation, style, or pattern) to guide us through the labyrinth and jungle called life. Guilt, which we are unaware of, often comes from our parents' teachings of what is right or wrong. It is very difficult to handle and requires revising our belief system and how we use those interpretations appropriately in new life situations.

When people look at the next generation, they are surprised and wonder why this generation is completely different. Each generation is different because the previous generation failed to adapt their belief system to the new situation. However, it is not necessary to always challenge beliefs and give others the chance to return to the old forgotten and more functional interpretations of basic beliefs.

SHAME

Shame is a very close feeling to guilt and also produces negative thinking that is based on a distortion in a person's thoughts. Instead of concentrating on resolving the situation, revising his or her belief system and solving problems, this person concentrates on his or her feeling of shame, which do not represent the present situation. Sometimes thinking about the feeling of shame or fear to experience shame produces avoidance, social isolation, and inability to develop effective personal relationships, which often happens among very young, very old, or disabled people, which represent the groups of people with social inadequacies.

If we understand that each stage of our existence is a normal variation of life and accept this without self-confusion, self-diminishing, or self-rejection, we could be much happier, especially if being different is not our fault or choice, or a conflict with our belief system. This way of negative thinking supports eating disorders (anorexia nervosa and bulimia), somatization, or sexual dysfunction as a result of difficulty accepting our bodies; deviation from normal appearance; confusion in using interpretations of our belief system; concentrating only on our physical or psychological deviations from all known norms; or failing to understand that the definitions of norms are relative and not absolute.

Shyness

Shyness is one variation of diffidence and shame. Shyness is seeing oneself as insignificant, minimized in a way that deserves rejection, and humiliated. A person with the shyness type of negative thinking lacks self-respect without acknowledgement of self-worth, which does not agree with his or her excellent qualities. This category of thinking causes social discomfort and self-consciousness that this person attracts only negative attention, which frequently expresses itself as fear of looking absurd, ridiculous, or inappropriate, or deserving laughter, contempt, rejection, jokes, humiliation, despise, etc.

This person uses social comparison in a very dysfunctional way. Moreover, this person can also experience physical and psychological symptoms that severely affect his or her social life and personal relationships. Shyness is based on incorrect interpretations of the basic system of values: this person interprets the superfluous value of each small detail that he or she misses in his or her behavior according to his or her understanding of the main belief system.

This person is characterized by an unjustified vision of him—or herself as a deviation from the conventional ideal and norms of society without any evidence of that conclusion, and thereby is distinguished from shame for something that affected or was not suitable to the public model; this defines the difference between shyness and shame. Absolutely normal, as society requires, a person experiencing shyness has a very low opinion of him—or herself and rejects or diminishes his or her merits and values, which declines the person's self-importance and in turn produces discomfort, confusion, and inadequacy, thereby limiting achievements in reaching goals and satisfaction in meeting his or her own needs.

Self-Criticism

Self-criticism expresses a form of negative thinking that reflects unconstructive defeating self-descriptions and statements that reveal a person's diminished qualities without evidence or facts of the person's achievements or development. As a result, it disqualifies the good points about us, big or small.

Self-criticism is negative observations and commentary from within us in our self-talk about our actions and patterns of behavior. When you ask the opinion of your internal critic and, in this case, experience heavy pangs of conscience, tortured feelings, and self-humiliation with hatred for yourself, this is self-criticism, which in a negative sense of the word also includes incorrect interpretation of the basic system of values.

Self-criticism, in the accurate sense, intends prevention and correction of incorrect interpretations of the basic system of values and implies averting deviations from all known principles and rules.

The use of positive and less rigid schemas of what is true and what is mistaken is one way to reduce the negative impact of excessive self-criticism. If you suggest that your personality represents the normal version of standards instead of a whole range of shortcomings, then it is possible to more easily control your inner critic, improve self-confidence, and find comfort with who you are.

Self-criticism also belongs to social comparison and perfectionism—negative ways of thinking that reflect criticism not only under the influence of real events but frequently under the effect of fictitious, distorted, and unrealistic circumstances, as well as imaginable and untrue negative states and conditions of people. Selfcriticism normally suggests in reality the development of normal adaptation and reasonable correction of thinking and behavior, along with healthy implication of social comparison, and improvement and evolution of our own personalities in an enhanced way. But if we overdo this, if we have been overzealous and exaggerated, we punish ourselves in a very unpleasant way, which prevents us from succeeding and accomplishing our essential goals.

NORAH LANG

HUMILIATION

This type of negative thinking includes thoughts of inadequacy, shame, rejection, embarrassment, deprivation of honor, and unjustified charges. Together with fact, humiliation reflects suffering and torture without the feeling of guilt that we are bad and made a mistake. This thinking connects with other people's hatred for us and expresses feelings of extreme pain without feeling guilt for something we didn't do wrong. However, this thinking of humiliation reflects projection of extreme disapproval and unjustified criticism by other people without any good evidence or proof. The thoughts and feelings of humiliation contribute to our realization of ourselves as victims of injustice in our own eyes; as victims, we have been hurt and unfairly criticized, which often leads to thoughts of revenge and fantasies about payback with the same painful injury that we have been experiencing. This thinking of humiliation is frequently an inadequate and excessive response to the situation.

This is the kind of reaction that reflects preliminary experience with humiliating factors that remind us of sorrowful events and feelings hidden in the corners of our subconscious memories. The exaggerated thoughts and feelings can arouse hate, offense, rage, and anger, which often stir up recollections of abuse in childhood and mockeries in past situations when we were dependent and powerless that resemble the present-life situations. This type of thinking requires a lot of courage, self-esteem, control, love for self, and professional support to eliminate the unpleasant consequences of humiliation, which are incompatible with revenge, that can force us to feel guilty for causing hurt and harm to others who can bring damage to our self-esteem, confirm our negative self-image, and confirm the insignificance of our personalities. Becoming like our offenders, we don't make right, fair, or beautiful choices. It makes us the same ugly, unfair, untruthful, and bad people as those who humiliated us. This also brings on isolation, mistrust, deepened pain, and misfortune more and more. It converts us to almost animals and reduces us in our own and other people's eyes. Only by forgetting and forgiving offenses can we gain moral victory in the eyes of offenders, and our own dignity. Moreover, we assert beauty, cleanliness, humanism, and wisdom.

Low Self-Esteem

Low self-esteem is a frequent form of negative thinking that takes from us freedom in our actions and limits our success in life. In other words, this thinking includes thoughts that we don't deserve, love, respect, or place. This occurs when people neglect to give us praise or recognition of our merits. When we cannot be satisfied by our achievements, we feel guilty, reduced, and uncertain in our acts. We always find deficiencies and errors in ourselves and compare ourselves to other people, less to our own benefit and with self-underestimation.

Generally, this thinking reflects a constant and distorted form of the social comparison type of negative thinking—comparing oneself to the qualities and merits of other people, without objective estimation of one's own abilities and achievements. In this way, low self-esteem is thinking about taking excessive responsibility; self-blame every time we are criticized by other people; and elements of exceeded guilt, self-condemnation, and unjustified observation.

It means pliability of our own rights and giving up under small pressure, which is necessary for us without resistance to other people's demands and requests. It includes inability to meet our own needs and expectation of help and support from others in situations we can easily handle on our own. In this case, we can't believe in ourselves or our abilities and prefer instead to entrust tasks to other people rather than taking into account our own opinions. We always expect approval and support instead of taking our own actions to resolve problems. Therefore, we can't come to a decision, and we follow other people's advice, ignoring our own experience in meeting our essential needs. Moreover, we are indecisive when other people expect resoluteness and effectiveness. In the end, we defeat all our hopes and interests. Finally, we prefer to remain in the hands of fate and depend on other people's choices. As a result, we will sink into our doubts and uncertainty.

Hopelessness

Hopelessness also represents a very unpleasant feeling and supports negative thinking that reflects lack of hope and sometimes generates thoughts of suicide. A very funny short story by Anton Chekhov contains advice for people who are thinking about suicide: if you cut your finger, be happy it is not your eye; if your wife is not faithful to you, be happy that she didn't betray your country…, etc. In one Italian romantic movie, a young man declared to his rich, much older mistress that he intended to kill himself with the purpose of making her suffer and feel indelible pain. She responded that she would not remember it for long and would forget it all in the near future, which would be much sooner than he thought. This stopped him from committing suicide.

Loss of hope is similar to loss of motivation—the absence of taste for life. In the afore mentioned short story, "White Nights," by Fyodor Dostoyevsky, the hero imagined exquisite, pleasant images and fantastic scenes of life in situations when he had no hope for happiness. Hope and imagination of different wishful images and scenes help us keep going and have motivation to challenge life, survive in sad and hopeless situations, and turn them into happiness as a result of our own activities and patience. Young people frequently don't have any idea why and for what they are living, and unfortunately they have suicidal thoughts.

They can't solve their problems, and instead of focusing on resolving them, they concentrate on their psychological pain. The answer to doubts and tortures in feelings of hopelessness is in the fact that sooner or later the situation will pass, and the bright day of hope will come after a dark night. We can prevent all of the world's catastrophes by applying our creative minds and science. It is the only way to fulfill our needs and desires. If our dreams sometimes go in the wrong direction and become unrealistic, we can chose other more real and pleasant options instead of feeling disappointment and hopelessness.

PROJECTION

Projection is another form of negative thinking that is expressed in two ways.

In the first subtype, we can project our own opinions about ourselves or our motivations for other people. In this instance, we assume that we have been doing something incorrectly and giving other people (who think as badly about us as we do) the wrong impressions, according to our own opinion and estimation of our actions. If we see ourselves as rejected, unlovable, miserable, and pathetic, other people might think about us in the same way. We hide with this version of negative thinking and unconsciously imply our dislike and disappointments in ourselves, which we ascribe to other people's feelings and thoughts. Jokes about issues such as racist views, sex, homosexuality, or any other concepts can express fear before the disclosure of our own internal contradictions. The censure of other people for mistakes, bad habits, or manners can be an unconscious manifestation of self-blaming in the same defects. We can predict ideas about the future thoughts and behaviors others, but they don't find conformation in reality because of the negative projection of our own opinions about other people.

The second subtype and implications of similar negative thinking can be assumed when people attack us unreasonably and groundlessly because they are sure in the fact that they understand and foresee our thoughts and behavior (often negatively). The origin of this confidence occurs from distant experiences in childhood when our parents spread ideas like everything must be correct or incorrect, which departs to the unconscious part our reasoning and determines the tendencies in our thinking and behavior. These people predict our feelings and thinking on the basis of their own concealed unconscious desires and motivations, which do not reflect realistic explanations in each situation and which produce the experience of the projection type of negative thinking.

Mixing Thought with Fact

The idea behind the adoption of thought for fact is another dysfunctional form of negative thinking that reflects general human error or a mental condition when wishful thinking becomes reality in the consciousness. If our imagination goes far beyond the limits of the probable and accessible, it borders on folly or insanity. It disrupts the principles of the natural course and normal life process, and then it is possible to speak about mixing thought with fact. This type of negative thinking includes other negative forms: exaggeration, jumping to conclusions, egocentrism, overgeneralization, projection, double standards, etc. When we sincerely believe without reason that our thoughts reflect reality, we inevitably come to irrational thinking and similar mixing of thoughts with fact.

In this case, we believe that thinking is what happened with us in real life; we are assured that our thoughts are generated by real facts and possible events. We are confident that our thoughts are real facts and possible developments that we calculated and invited for correctional works through our "extraordinary minds" and believed without a serious or objective test. We exaggerate reality in a wrong and mistaken way that causes us and other people problems and troubles as a result of our devised, grandiose ideas. We act unrealistically. We crush and disappoint other people. We predict unreal future events that are not natural results in continuation and don't progress in imagining anything. We are hurried about conclusions on the basis of a hypothesis about the involvement of different people in different situations, as well was our own roles, without taking into account scientific substantiation, natural laws, and adequate information.

Unconsciously, this person can project his or her own fears and wishes onto other people who never planned to do anything similar. This person creates his or her own rules for other people, which he follows, mixing thinking with unreal life situations, predispositions, and his or her understanding of how things need to be. He or she is building a fictional reality based on his or her thoughts, consistently constructing a picture of the world without taking into account realistic explanations or other people's opinions and experiences. When a person imagines unbelievable success in the future and leads others to nowhere, that also produces bad consequences and reflects negative thinking: mixing thought with fact. This is supported by negative thinking, which reflects mental symptoms such as bipolar disorder with maniacal symptoms or cases of schizophrenia or schizoid personality disorder.

Predicting the Future

When we become zealous in predicting the future rather than being reasonable and realistic, we are experiencing a type of negative thinking called predicting the future. If we predict only bad things, we can fall into serious depression or other mental conditions, and if our brains continue to be in this state for a long time, this blocks our best ability to solve problems correctly.

It seems more sensible to have an idea that bad things might happen, but displaying our ability to focus on the resolution of these problems might be better. If we don't think about the inevitable and possible predictions, we can put enough effort into resolving problems step-by-step by dividing them into very small parts without focusing on alerting negative results. This gives us the strength and consciousness to mobilize our best abilities better, and real problems disappear gradually.

Predicting the future becomes urgent when combined with a state of obsessive compulsive disorder, which produces dysfunctional thinking and behavior; it is further complicated by ritual actions meant to prevent even small possibilities of predicted danger. A very good example of this behavior is the hero of Anton Chekhov's famous short story "The Man in a Shell," who carried an umbrella in sunny weather, checked the lock on the door countless times, and returned home numerous times under the suspicion that something irreparable and terrible had happened. Predictions of horrors and expectations of misfortunes in the future are part of the manifestation of panic attacks and generalized anxiety disorder. Terrifying things are also imagined by patients with post-traumatic stress disorder.

Jumping to Conclusions

Jumping to conclusions is a form of negative thinking that relates to many other types of negative thinking. It can be a gateway for many other irrational forms of conclusions. In this case, we can assume negative means and events, without evidence of being rejected, criticized, ignored, humiliated; blaming; feeling shame or guilt; thinking of revenge; experiencing projection, social inadequacy, or discomfort; mixing fact with thought; concentrating on one mistake; condemning oneself and others on the basis of a single event; expecting of punishment; or taking excessive responsibility as a result of one suspicious sign or hint of something similar from a previous sad experience.

Without doubts, we jump to conclusions as a result of our dysfunctional and irrational interpretations of events, words, or actions, or we imagine something bad, or we predict or read other people's minds. We can become angry and do things we regret for our entire lives, things that can't be undone. We need to stop concentrating on negative thinking and instead analyze positive explanations. First, we should always suggest an encouraging alternate explanation and then collect more information, evidence, and data to support our assurance that our original negative hypothesis is indeed incorrect. This will prevent us from jumping to conclusions and burning bridges, or help us restore relationships or damages that resulted from wrong conclusions.

Using Ultimatum Words

The use of ultimatum words like *always, never, everyone, everything*, and *nothing* frequently brings into play negative thinking that reflects exaggeration and unconstructive focus. This usually happens when a person manipulates the expression of a situation by offering absolute and rigid conclusions as the only exceptionally correct options and ignores other positive and objective explanations and interpretations.

This type of negative thinking is also very similar to overgeneralization and magnification and minimization, which reflect conclusions based on a small number of facts or a distorted imagination; these types of negative thinking exclude more neutral or positive perceptions of the world, people, facts, events, and conceptions. *Always* indicates a word that means an underestimation of the significance of some facts and an exaggeration of others, which means a person is inclined to jump to one conclusion only. *Never* is a word that excludes any chance of changing or challenging anything now or in future and diminishes the possibility and hope of making a difference.

EXCESSIVE RESPONSIBILITY

Exaggerated responsibility is a frequent type of negative thinking that displays a person's wrong idea about the fact that he or she must make it all by him—or herself. Taking excessive responsibility means exaggerating a person's obligation to do everything, which is required of him or her more and more. It is expressed by taking excessive responsibility for tasks and putting in more effort to obtain only positive and perfect results and make it so that everyone is content. In other words, a person's goal is to satisfy every desire and need for everyone, and to seriously fulfill every request and demand of other people. This person can't abide any failure and frequently experiences other forms of negative thinking like selfblame, self-criticism, self—hatred, self-humiliation, diminishing self-worth, perfectionism, expecting approval, social comparison, and expecting punishment, which contribute to the development of his or her mental condition.

If this person operates with healthy reactions, he or she would accept the fact of new experiences and natural human errors, which might prevent him or her from jumping to conclusions about his or her responsibility and negative results. It would also not interfere with sharing his or her difficulties with others; setting limits and boundaries; talking openly about his or her limitations without shame or fear of displeasing others; or concentrating on his or her successes, abilities, and possibilities, as well as positive experiences and results. It is necessary to be rational and daring when acknowledging limitations in actual possibilities, without exaggeration and overgeneralization of the role and value of failure. It is also necessary to be commensurate to other new circumstances without confusion about one's own "mistaken identity," which refers to the assumption of having made a insignificant error that is incorrectly categorized as a complete failure.

PESSIMISM

Pessimism is a type of negative thinking that is more frequently encountered in young people when they can't explain contradictions and disharmony in the world; why humanity composes rules and laws but then makes many exceptions and corrections to them; and why humanity designs a society in which it is necessary to wear different masks, pretend, simulate, and play multiple roles and games so that those exceptions can work.

The famous pessimist Schopenhauer developed his pessimistic theory in his early twenties, and it expresses nihilism, which rejects the existing world and the structure of society. Pessimism is a negative vision of the world that depicts general reality as a continuous negative panorama of life, completely drawing a solitary negative idea and concentrating heavily on its negative aspects. This form of negative thinking supports suicidal thoughts, causes depression, and rejects the possibility of enjoyment in life.

Pessimists focus on negative explanations only, taking into account proof of negative outcomes and blindly excluding other positive sides of reality and our existence. The opposite of pessimism is optimism, which is developed in older people, whose years overflow with the desire to live and appreciate every moment of their existence, no matter how painful it is, even with diseases, which cause torture and suffering. After reading this book, young people can realize that disharmony in their feelings can be corrected by challenging distortions in thinking in order to increase pleasurable, real, and successful shifts in life, which can be free of confusion and disappointment.

AUTOMATIC NEGATIVE THINKING

Automatic thoughts represent all thoughts that are formed unconsciously from our basic beliefs and can't be explained. We don't know
why, when, or how these thoughts are brought to our attention.
Sometimes these thoughts are heard and seen in our consciousness so
much that we can't develop awareness of new information, circumstances, facts, and situations, which become unnoticed and ignored
by our minds.

When automatic thoughts torment us, we are absolutely sure
of their true and absolute truthfulness, without doubts about their
deceiving nature. We mix up our beliefs with real facts. We jump to
conclusions and automatic thoughts, which are produced as a result
of distortions and illusions in our minds. Those thoughts jump out
of hidden corners in our minds to our attention and play us out like
a bad game, pulling the strings that deceive our interests. Sometimes
it comes to a point that we can't consider them thoroughly, and this

is expressed as irrational and dysfunctional actions and behaviors that we will regret. Later we realize our actions as mistakes, shortages, and blunders, and we are surprised at their origins. And if we are not aware of the automatic nature of our conceived thoughts, which come from a distorted and dysfunctional subconscious belief system, as they affect our actions and behavior, we will repeat these mistakes over and over.

Acknowledging the automatic roots and origins of this kind of negative thinking is big progress in controlling negative thinking and bringing it into balance with standards of behavior. For this we should remodel our schemas of thinking according to new situations and new information in order to revise our belief system to produce fast responses more adequately and appropriately, without distorted thinking and behavior. The need for constant and flexible revision of our main ideas and beliefs is obvious. Such revision must be without conclusions and reactions that are rigid and poorly constructed in reality, which can be quite experimental and a vital lesson in real-life situations.

DISTORTED NEGATIVE THINKING

Distorted negative thoughts are those that appear in our minds in order to protect, prevent, and meet devised and unrealistic dreams and desires that can't be true in nature and logic, do not reflect reality, and are not logically correct. Distorted thoughts can be fantastic dreams and obvious nonsense driven by sensitive content without logical substantiation (emotional reasoning), which can affect a personality's ability to function in society, fulfill needs, set and reach goals, produce serious problems, and request professional help. This thinking lacks logic and reflects confusion and cloudiness in the mind. This can be seen in a person's symbolic, distorted belief system, which manifests itself in conversation, actions, and behavior.

Along with this, the distorted form of negative thinking can be less obvious and can be expressed in unclear, irrational forms that represent all kinds of negative thinking in very organized (in some points of view) actions and in specific stages. However, these forms produce other more distractive problems, confusion, or deviations in thinking and behavior. But at the same time, this thinking—even though it is obscured and covered by the devised diagram—remains in content mostly irrational, illogical, and contradictory to the basic belief system. This thinking can be compared to a reflection in a curved mirror, in which real-world images become very different and distorted. This thinking reflects a distorted mirror image of reality. It is expressed in the complex group of all enumerated and described types of negative thinking in this book, or in some of them together, or in only one of them—and only in the most dysfunctional way.

DYSFUNCTIONAL NEGATIVE THINKING (UNHELPFUL NEGATIVE THINKING)

Dysfunctional or unhelpful negative thoughts sound logically correct and reflect our basic belief system. However, at the same time, they don't reflect the changes of a new reality or exceptional situations that produce severe dysfunctions in society. This is a frequent form of negative thinking when entering into a contradiction of the evidences and experiences we acquire periodically in all stages of our lives. The healthy type of thinking implies understanding limitations, possibilities, and changes in new life situations, based on our basic belief system. Flexibility is a necessary skill in order to be reconstructed and accommodated according to a new reality and a new main belief system based on a background of logical thinking. This is a necessary condition for the realization of our plans and basic vital tasks, as well as our dreams and desires. It is the main remedy for logical consumptions and the only way to make everything, or at least most parts of life, work in the way we imagined.

New experiences and new facts reject many concepts, which over the course of time become dysfunctional and antiquated. This forced society to step back from many religious concepts and to revise them in the present time. That doesn't make it right to put too much faith in remodeling and taking other illogical directions in our development of new concepts. It goes without saying that it should not be the rule to thoughtlessly trust revision of all values in illogical directions; this is not the solution to problems in functional thinking. Instead, we are required to constantly match consistency in our thinking with practical new experiences, without excessive and corrupted deviations from our basic belief system and main values, which are developed by the millennial knowledge of humanity. Revision and reconstruction in the direction of our thinking does not exclude returning to old, long-time-approved values if this is reasonable at any time, because these values have long served as direction and a guide through centuries of this test and labyrinth called life.

PLAUSIBLE NEGATIVE THINKING

Plausible negative thinking can be present in different versions of negative thinking, and it is very similar to positive thinking, but it produces negative results. The positive content of those thoughts can be unrealistic and dysfunctional. The reverberation positivity and information in these thoughts can contribute to other negative ways of thinking that affect our lives and functioning, such as exaggeration, overgeneralization, jumping to conclusions, mixing thought with fact, egocentrism, etc.

Plausible negative thinking reflects poor judgment, incorrect conclusions, distorted thinking, and dysfunctional assumptions and involves many confusions and contradictions in real-life situations. If someone offers us very pleasing proposals and we do not consider them thoroughly or match them to our own reality, then we are in very ambiguous, difficult, and unpleasant situations. If we do the same with our own imagination of the plausible situation, don't match it to our experience, and make the wrong choice, we can pay a very big price later. In this case, we make an incorrect selection and an erroneous decision with all the consequences emerging for us, and we deceive ourselves.

We need to constantly match our own and other people's experiences, as well model our experiences on art, books, movies, television shows, newspaper stories—any reasonable sources of information for our thinking that seem plausible for our productive interpretation of their pleasant and desirable content.

INVOLUNTARY NEGATIVE THINKING

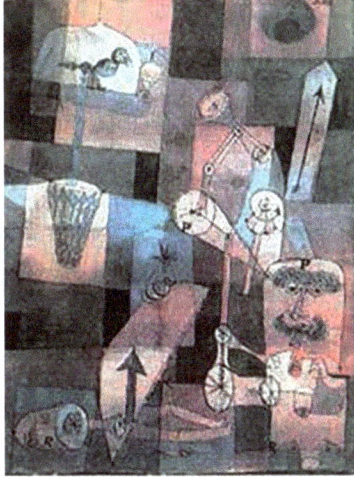

Involuntary negative thinking resembles an automatic way of thinking, but it is differed in that it is not built on and does not occur in the system of values, rules, fixed childhood experiences, or habits in thoughts and behavior. It is based on our exceptional needs and instincts, and we are in constant contradiction with our own rules and society's requirements, which complicate our observation of what we believe or want to believe, especially when such thoughts come as inexplicable and strong desires that alter the part that goes with our faith.

Thoughts like that unconsciously pop up in our attention from time to time. We can be surprised at how our thoughts and actions are contradictive when we experience this type of negative thinking. We unconsciously protect those thoughts and adapt our basic rules and beliefs in ways that make it easy to reimburse them. We create complicated behavior and wear many masks to realize the involuntary thoughts. If we are aware of them and learn to control this negative way of thinking, we will bring our behavior into balance with our own rules and beliefs, as well as society's requests and human logic, and correctly apply them in our real-life situations. Then our actions will comply with the main system of values and basic beliefs.

CHAPTER VI

MODIFICATION OF
THINKING AND BEHAVIOR

The previous chapter presented ideas about changes in basic and other beliefs and the corresponding negative ways of thinking that are reflected unfavorably in our behavior and psychological problems. It was intended to reexamine our belief system or views and replace them with something more adaptive and functional. However, in this case, the chapter suggests a flexible enough strategy for the return to the previous belief system, which under special and new circumstances could not satisfy the basic principle of survival, or would produce conflict between different beliefs and values.

At the same time, this strategy remains problematic as we change basic beliefs to more functional and correct interpretations of them. This implies experimenting and selecting more adequate interpretations of our belief system and creating harmonious thinking and behavior, which in turn can act only under specified conditions and in a specific period that doesn't exclude returning to previous values that are checked by through our long-time system of values.

The contradiction of this kind of implication is in the right choice of changes without regret of leaving old beliefs behind, until the time is right to return to them. Many different techniques have been developed to modify negative thinking, underlying beliefs, and dysfunctional behavior and to facilitate psychological problems. The remarkable fact is that we are comfortable with our dysfunctional thinking and content with our irrational beliefs and usually resist changing of our behavioral patterns.

Young, dynamic people very quickly grasp the necessity of changing their system of views to new modes or new forms of thinking and behavior that represent existent changes of their present lifestyles. This exclusively and exceptionally distinguishes them from the preexistent generation. All other people with so-called traditional views on contemporary changes are very slow in awareness of the new dynamic of life, and they require sufficiently precise proof that their thinking, beliefs, and behaviors are dysfunctional and need modification.

All of the above sounds like an impossible task with insurmountable difficulties, but it's not. In reality, there are methods that help us change our system of views, forms of thinking, and behavior. However, what helps this process? What helps is when we realize the necessity of the nature of change under the influence of irrefutable facts, or when other people call us to change and we come face-to-face with the reality of life or are astonished with desperation, which inevitability contributes to change. According to this, we need to be determined and committed, with a strong desire and harmonious need, in order to complete any change.

Again, we are not comfortable being forced, and nothing can come easily from negative emotions; on the contrary, it must come from our inspiration and enthusiasm, which emanates from the positive side of our minds. That is when we willingly and efficiently make changes. But how do we find inspiration?

We should use positive imagination, which is based on past positive recollections of experiences and images that contain similar positive changes from the past. As part of this, we must take into account realistic data and focus on attempts and the positive results of these attempts without exaggeration or regrets. We must also understand the objective limitations and possibility of errors in our actions in case of failure.

The rest of this chapter is dedicated to explaining techniques to accomplish change in our system of views, forms of thinking, and behavior.

DISTRACTION

This technique is effective at the beginning of the process to modify our thinking and behavior, prior to beginning fundamental changes. These distracting actions and occupations predetermine switching at the positive, neutral, and relaxing moments in life, which reflect a normal functioning range. Anything that distracts us from negative thinking can be beneficial. The following activities are one of my patient's ideas of a good time:

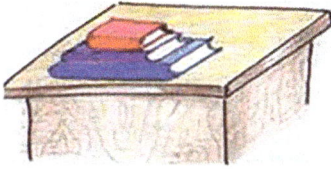

reading books

meeting friends
going to parties

fishing

Dancing

playing chess and sports

walking on the beach
and other places

traveling

surfing on the computer   playing videogames   listening to our
                                                   playing music

going to restuarants or preparing   attending theaters, shoes,
dinner parties at home   concerts, and movies

knitting and making things

painting and visiting galleries

gardening

taking care of pets and animals

Ideas for a good time can be diverse in correspondence with the preferences of different people.

Problem-Solving Techniques

An interesting procedure for reducing negative thinking can serve as a problem-solving technique which lead to the selection of a series of alternative solutions that help resolve problems.

The most important step when beginning to use this technique is to define and list all consistent problems. It can be useful to divide larger problems into a set of small problems, which will help determine the most possible (alternative) and optimal solutions and will predetermine more chances to resolve the primary problem. Solutions to problems depend on one's habits, lifestyle, and preparedness for changes in thinking and behavior, which no longer work for this person in the specified conditions.

In the beginning, it is necessary to focus on efforts and attempts to change. If we remember that we can advance forward toward our purpose using the step-by-step technique, and if we encourage ourselves toward any positive outcome, this will be the correct strategy in any complicated situation and lead to a consequent solution. This will gradually become our basic direction.

We need to understand that sometimes we might fail, but if we feel good about the many attempts we have made, this can support our self-confidence, which is also part of the problem-solving technique. It is sometimes necessary to seek the professional help and support of a psychologist, or to talk to relatives and friends, gather exact data, and make corrections in our sources of knowledge for resolving problems; these actions are also part of the problem-solving technique. In the course of searching for the right solution, we can figure out alternate plans for each problem: plan A, plan B, etc.

RELATIONSHIP PROBLEMS

Building any relationship is a difficult and complex task for the majority of people. The solution to relationship problems bears vital needs that reflect the importance of success in the completion of our whole life purpose. Everyone needs to develop healthy relationships with other people. This need is defined by the basic purpose of creating our own families, having children, and securing and ensuring that we have throughout our lives the attention, love, consideration, and support of the people and family around us, especially at critical moments like illness, old age, social distress, etc.

This purpose is so important that it obviously reflects all efforts of any human and is expressed in the varied actions and behaviors we perform to complete this task successfully. Subconsciously, humans take different directions to complete problematic tasks; in some cases these directions reflect different types of dysfunctional thinking and behavior that affect their own and other people's lives. All of the above can be reasonable in setting some essential goals and resolving individual problems with alternative resolutions according to specific life situations.

Motivation in different relationships reflects trends in future children's improved genetic, social, and psychological features through natural selection in any society at any time. This is based on sexual and social preferences and improvement in the quality and duration of healthy lives for oneself, one's family, and one's community.

Those tendencies are implicit of better survival instincts, including the selection of the best partner with whom to have children. Those children's genetics can improve physical, social, and psychological survival features. Because each human being is part of a community and can't survive alone, mating became an essentially important purpose in life.

Alternative solutions for relationship problems

- Acquire social and communication skills by using role-playing and modeling techniques.
- Develop a healthy lifestyle that includes physical exercise, a healthy diet, involvement in pleasurable activities, etc.
- Broaden your experiences.
- Strengthen social and personal bonds with other people. These bonds can include openness, trust, having fun together, mutual understanding, flexibility, cooperation, personal growth, love, consideration, etc.
- Improve your verbal expression in communication; remember some discretion in verbalization, and the value of silence.
- Make clear things that can be changed in order to make this relationship work.
- Acknowledge your own and other people's limitations and abilities, and learn to accept them.
- Coordinate your assertiveness with other people's interests, avoid conflicts and arguments, pay attention to others, and try to fulfill your own and other people's needs in healthy ways.

HEALTH PROBLEMS

A healthy lifestyle includes complex thoughts, actions, habits, and patterns behavior that reflect education from a person's family and society, physical and psychological development of genetic features, healthy diet, and good medical care. Chinese remedies and natural food often compete with the recommendations of science, which sometimes contradict the natural balance in the physical condition of the body; produce side effects, drug interactions, and dependency; and suppress the body's defense mechanisms. This can lead to the development of new health problems that affect normal functioning to one degree or another in all areas, including psychological functioning. Special diets, restrictions, and limitations in nourishment produce a lack of essential nutrients and promote other medical problems; this is a warning for special diet lovers. Limitations in meat can produce anemia, osteoporosis, muscle and joint weakness, which can be signs of cancer.

Limitations in fatty food can lead to a deficiency of vitamins, other kinds of depletion, dementia, and infections, which can also be signs of cancer. Carbohydrates are essential to our strength, mood, energy production, bones, joints, blood vessels, and hearts. However, carbohydrates should not include sweets, cholesterol-rich products, or excessively starchy foods. All nourishing products need to be consumed in balanced quantities, and special diets should be only for people with medical conditions who are under the care of doctors.

Excessive exercise and extreme sport exertions can also promote future diseases and lead to injuries with risk of disability. These activities need to be balanced with appropriate nutrition and medical recommendations. Supplements (vitamins, minerals, herbs, etc.) can be a solution for a lack of natural food or time to prepare healthy food, or the inability to establish adequate attention in maintaining a balanced diet. In instances treating illnesses with antibiotics when there is no viral infection, Acidophilus Plus supplements are a good solution; they are available in all natural health stores and support useful bacteria (microflora in our mouths, stomachs, bowels, skin, and genitals) that have protected our bodies from different infections since we were born (excluding patients with immune-compromised diseases who are susceptible to normal flora in developing certain diseases). These microflora have been attacked by our diets, antibiotics, and other medications throughout our lives.

Good hygiene is an essential factor of health. Having fun and rest every day are too. Sleeping for seven hours, give or take an hour or two, is also very important for our bodies.

Alternative solutions for health problems

- Establish a healthy diet and lifestyle.
- Take supplements and make time for physical exercise.
- Follow good personal hygiene.
- Obtain the resources to pay for health care.
- Find a good physician you trust, gain a second opinion, or research information on the Internet about your medical problem. Be sure to use medical help only when appropriate, without exaggerating your problems.
- Report side effects of medications and reduce dosage of medications only under the care and control of a doctor.

PROBLEMS STUDYING

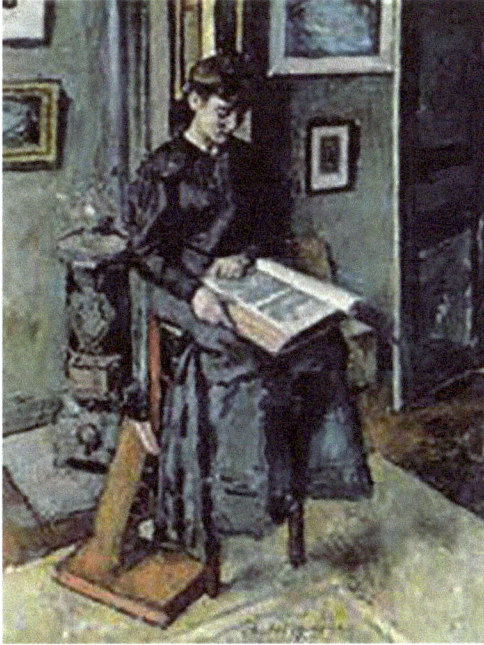

Education can be a big problem because of the inability to retain information and study. Memory is an amazing ability that allows us to accumulate, store, and use appropriate information in the course of daily activities according to the requirements of our communities and our need to gain professional skills in a field of knowledge. People with good memories sometimes lack the appropriate attention spans and concentration to accumulate information and are therefore unable to use that information accordingly in future situations. They can't organize their time, and they often become involved in an excessive quantity of distracting activities.

Some people with good memories, attention spans, and concentration are unable to extract main ideas and make correct conclusions because they are too focused on the little details and facts, which shield the whole picture with excessive information. A number of people have selective memory, which manifests into the ability to memorize or pay attention only to interesting subjects and facts without attaching value to other components that are unremarkable to their points of view; this can negatively affect test scores and grades despite the fact that these people are able to understand main ideas and use them practically in the future. They have gaps in their knowledge that make them seem illiterate, but this is the wrong impression.

The idea of education is not to know everything or perfect the concepts, which are in reality undefined. It is impossible to embrace the immense information pool or know each small detail and fact in every region of knowledge. It is only possible to concentrate on effort, constant recollection, and use of correct conclusions and analysis. These are tools in effective studying. Missing information and steps in school and college or other educational programs can be irreversible in time and one's ability to acquire certain qualifications and professional knowledge in different areas of science. They are revised constantly according to new standard levels of knowledge.

Alternative solutions to studying problems

- Correctly organize your time and the distribution of your daily tasks according to priority.
- Concentrate mostly on efforts rather than achievements or results. Study the more interesting subjects and information first, focusing on their usefulness in the future.
- Repeatedly recollect routines and information in all available slots of time in order to successfully pass exams.
- Revise and compare old and new information with facts, experiences, and other precise sources of information.
- Don't be ashamed to ask questions or disclose your incompetence on subjects that other informed people know better.
- Show your knowledge at first, and don't repress your opinion easily.
- Check serious sources of information regarding confusing or debatable facts.
- Gain new information constantly so you don't lose time.

- Hire a tutor or go to classes for improvement in your educational level and to restore missed stages in the knowledge.
- Choose the field of knowledge you like the most and that will be your preference for study in the future.
- Set attainable goals in your studies, and appropriate payment for your education.
- Complete studying and other educational tasks daily. Don't leave anything for tomorrow that you can do today. But at the same time, be reasonable

CAR ACCIDENTS

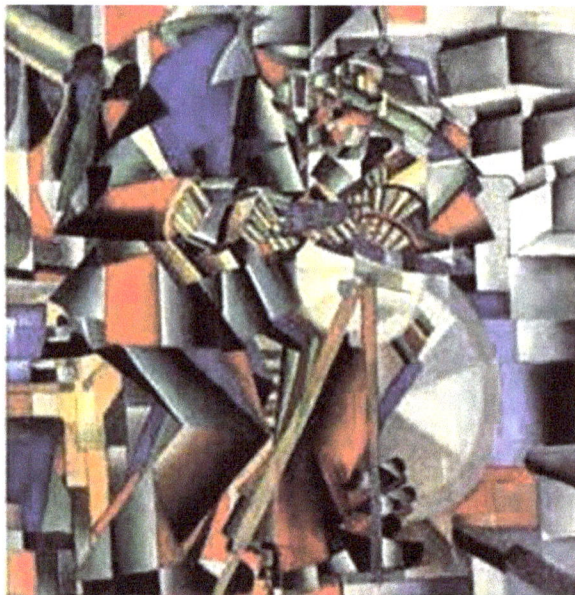

All accidents promote stress, and it is possible to subsequently develop psychological problems. Driving is a vital need in some areas. It helps improve quality of life and establishes higher standards of living in the sped-up rhythm of civilization. It also defines a person's level of functioning.

However, car accidents occur and contribute to different psychological problems including post-traumatic stress disorder, panic attacks, general anxiety, fear of driving, etc. One thought about a possible car accident can support fear and withdrawal from driving for a long time. Going to therapy can help, along with abstraction from thoughts, which cause fears. Additional helpful techniques include distracting and relaxation exercises; positive imagery; and replacing negative ways of thinking like predicting the future, pessimism, guilt, blaming, low self-esteem, catastrophization, exaggeration, etc. Inspiring facts can include the number of surviving drivers and any person who was in a car accident and returned to driving without fear or further emergences in the future.

Alternative solution for car accident problems

- Learn carefully the reliable habits of safe driving.
- Follow driving rules and give attention, caution, and respect to road signs.
- Don't take alcohol and drugs that affect driving.
- It is sometimes better to resort to public transportation if you are at risk of an emergency during driving.
- Don't talk on the phone while driving.
- Make sure you know the way to your destination; avoid using a navigation device when possible.
- Verify any vision or medical status that might affect your driving with a doctor.
- Remember that rushing and driving at high speeds is one cause of car accidents.
- Respect other drivers and pedestrians on the road.
- Check traffics rules and changes regularly.
- Remember, after an accident you need to be careful but in a sensible way, without fear of future driving.
- Some accidents are not your fault. Stop blaming yourself.
- Don't exaggerate the possibility of a car accident. Stop predicting the future.
- Have ideas of possible accidents but concentrate on reasonable efforts to prevent them.
- Resolve legal problems as soon as you can.
- Take it slow when returning to driving after a car accident.
- Imagine resolutions of each possible difficulty in driving after an accident.

Court Problems

Legal problems and judicial trials can also lead to possible psychological symptoms and negative experiences that require psychiatric control and psychotherapy. Legal conflicts can reflect circumstances such as child abuse, divorce, credit cards, mortgage, medical bills, loan payments, criminal activity, chemical dependency and addictions, arrests, etc.

Regarding the disruption of the law, to a larger degree it involves people with corrupted basic systems of values and reflects their poor judicial education in present society. Social services have been called upon to help these groups of people; however, they experience huge resistance and sometimes danger in their efforts to reduce unwanted activities and resolve psychological problems of those groups of people. Frequently, criminals who use nonfunctional and irrational interpretations of the basic system of values and negative explanations of the proceeding events need the aid of public services to support and revise their belief systems.

At first it is extremely necessary to establish an understanding of the basic system of values, which may lead to the breaking of the law as a consequence of psychological problems and the lack of coordination in society. It is also necessary to bring to a person's consciousness the relativity of some positions in society and the absoluteness of legislation. They must accept the facts of this disharmony, forgive themselves and others for the inability to hold the limitations as defined by the law, and find the correct methods of solving their problems within the framework of the law in order to achieve a basic concept of survival in society. Some personalities break rules not because they want to survive or ensure a good existence for themselves but because they have insufficient experiences, knowledge of the law and structure of society, and ability in interpretation and decision making skills in certain life situations.

Modification of thinking and behavior is the necessary method to correct errors in explanations of real data and events and to help people choose alternative solutions for existing problems, according to the law if possible. Criminals manipulate interpretations of the basic system of values in very unhealthy ways because of errors. The basic persuasion of criminal personalities is that if someone else breaks a law with impunity and gets away with it, they too have the right to make the same or larger disruption to the law of society, and not just with basic survival and existence or meeting essential needs as the serious justifying factor to their criminal activities. This is the wrong conclusion. Such personalities miss other healthy solutions to their problems; instead, they copy other levelheaded people (which allow deviations within reasonable limits) and take into account one way that worked in other circumstances but is easy to follow even in more wrong and dysfunctional levels of deviation and in an even more irrational criminal direction. Such crazy personalities copy other healthy people with high levels of irregularity and significant disruptions of core values and the legal system in their criminal activities.

Alternative solutions for court problems

- Accept responsibility for court resolutions and orders.
- Make attempts at revising your basic system of values.

- Learn to make correct decisions by collecting more precise information and data.
- Learn to adjust your own interest to the interests of other people, and take a prosocial position.
- State values that support behavior that correspond with the boundaries of the law.
- Choose alternative coping mechanisms to adapt to negative emotions like anger, frustration, helplessness, or depression and reduce potential risk of breaking the law.

MARITAL PROBLEMS

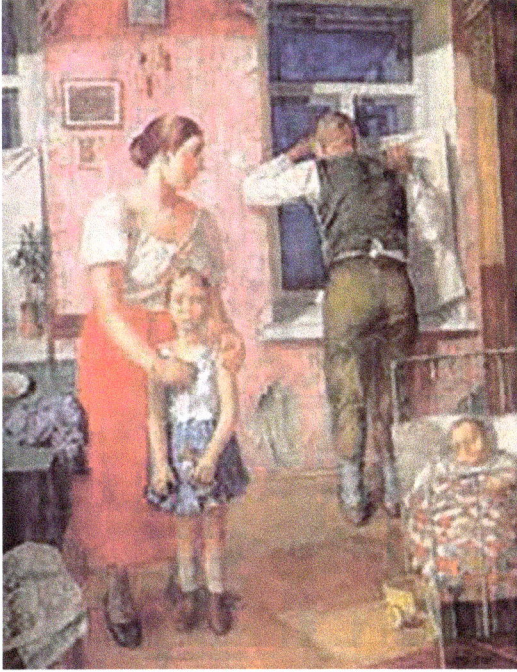

Marriage problems represent part of family problems and implicate the rights of each spouse to fulfill his or her main needs and desires in any way. In order to form a legal marriage, the commitment is based on the basic belief system and persuasions, which reflect the human needs of reproduction, sexuality, and survival. No matter how much trouble or how many tasks humans have in marriage, it remains the harmonious solution to establish the best existence in society. Because marriage involves greater financial responsibility for men, the commitment of marriage is much harder for them. At the same time, women have allotted in no small measure their own expectations in unrealistic dreams, which contradict and complicate many roles in their present marriages.

The traditional view of marriage is men pay the bills and women take care of the children and household chores. The ideals of marriage in contemporary society have changed, and that has produced marital problems. Men and women are building families based on the life experiences of their parents that they experienced during childhood. Together with that fact, contemporary families can inherit both the good and bad habits of their parents along with new habits that reflect the dynamics of current social relations. Sexual attraction and intellectual and spiritual equality are the best start for all marriages. Successful fusion with new roles and tasks produces new families and successful marriages. In the old days, most marriages were stable because the basic belief system was concordant to religious beliefs. Terrible conflicts and arguments didn't result in divorce even in marriages that were dysfunctional and only seemed happy.

Having children unites the spouses and was a very powerful strengthening force for marriage until sexuality took control and became an obsession as well as a main purpose of conjugal marital connections in contemporary society. Acknowledging the rights of women to healthy sex has been a destructive factor for many marriages in present reality. Extramarital affairs of both sides in relationships produce the main marital concerns in modern society. Freud and other psychodynamic promoters freed the human race from guilt of marital affairs, fear of sex, or problems that are based on sexual freedom in order to improve family and the institution of marriage.

But it is obvious that it is now time to establish equilibrium between the freedom of sex from guilt and the elimination of fear of sex according to the basic concepts of human values and relations, which continue to reflect the general disharmony of the world as determined by I. Mechnikov at the beginning of the XX century. It needs time to acknowledge how to follow the basic belief system while at the same time building healthy and functional marriages. Society has been divided into two groups: people who live in marriages and people who live alone, or other types of relationships that somehow coexist together.

Both groups are functional in present society and build the family structure in different ways. The majority of multicultural mediums (not including different religious cults and groups, or polygamists) are able to maintain a group of married people that are mostly based on the religious basis of matrimony. In the future, children who grew up with a single parent or with grandparents will struggle in their attempts to build healthy marriages and families. The interest of individuals to have the right of sexual selection frequently leads to divorces and the loss of one parent or the acquisition of a dysfunctional single parent, which is not concordant to the needs of children, who need the love and care of both parents in equal degrees. Divorced children's inharmonious ideas about family and marriage also sometimes complicate the building of better families and marriages in the future.

Diversions from the normal ideal marriage or family become more intense with the irreversible tendencies of modern society and the expectations of traditional society. There is no returning to the old absolute view of marriage and family. Along with this, new forms and deviations from the usual form of marriage and family (for example, gay marriage) are located in the stage of natural experiment. This produces contradictory results that show a high risk of failure and poor correspondence to real society. This is because the institution of traditional marriage was developed as an absolute alternative through the years in that traditional form, and the majority of people became accustomed it. This conclusion leaves one choice when considering the traditional forms of matrimony, family, and marriage, and also the problems connected with them.

Alternative solutions to marital problems

- Determine expectations and ideas about the marriage based on the experiences of others—for example, your parents and other married couples.
- Identify dysfunctional thinking and behaviors that have led to marital problems.
- Establish control over marital problems rather than leaving things to happen by chance or waiting for changes from the other partner.
- Don't force the change of your spouse. Speak clearly about your expectations and desires and make mutual concessions or bargain with each other.

- Concentrate on the motivations and attractions that led to this marriage.
- Find ways of stating your displeasure in a peaceful and calm way that displays assertiveness and control in talking about dissatisfactions in the marriage.
- Find activities and pleasure for both spouses, along with fulfilling everyday responsibilities together.
- Establish a dynamic, flexible approach in the distribution of responsibilities according to changes in situations and health of both spouses.
- Constantly reveal indicators of love and sympathy in your behavior, as well as verbalization.
- Refocus from recent arguments and conflicts, and pause in fighting without reminding each other of previous reasons that caused the conflict.
- Develop a tendency toward improvement in conjugal contacts and establish better communication with each other.
- Talk about satisfaction, not only concerns about problems.
- Encourage appropriate attempts to improve a spouse's behavior, but reasonably.
- Use positive imagination based on different sources (art, movies, books, recommendations of friends and professionals, etc.) to improve the marriage and the quality of time spent together.
- Acknowledge mental and medical problems and find professional help.
- Understand your and your spouse's limitations, learn to accept some of them, and be open to the opportunity to change in appropriate moments.
- Learn patience in listening to each other without domination or suppression.
- Forego changes that promote disagreement and distance.
- Concentrate on efforts rather than results for the improvement of the marriage.

GRIEF OF LOSS

Grief from the loss of a close person can happen with anyone, and over the course of time we normally resolve our pain and heal our wounds. But what happens if it does not pass easily and continues to darken our lives with the same intensity and strength as when it started? Acceptance of loss is the first and main step in resolving and dealing with grief. It is important to gradually become accustomed to a new lifestyle that inevitably changes after the loss. Thoughts about the excellent times we spent with the departed person can help quietly relieve the pain of our irreversible loss, and help us estimate our own roles in the lost person's life.

This is about overcoming pain caused by grief. It is a no less considerable process to follow the ritual grieving process of bidding farewell and mourning the loss of a loved one. Being distracted by the process and the many daily life activities is not noteworthy for this emotional state and dulls the pain of loss. Reversing life for other loving people is no less imperative in the healing process.

There are additional emotions and negative forms of thinking that reflect our grief that need revision and change: sadness, dependence on the departed person, feelings of being abandoned by the loved one, fear of being alone, guilt that is our fault, depression, lack of interest in life, lack of motivation, inability to make any change, worthlessness, hopelessness, predicting the future, panic attacks, anxiety, etc.

It is important to allow ourselves to feel happy again without guilt or blame, to focus on good thoughts about the lost person, and to keep memories about the good times we spent together. We need to commit to new happiness like we had before and get a new start. We should be surrounded by kind and loving people who give us support, consideration, and sympathy in this difficult cycle of life. We need to rest on the good we did for the person we lost and not blame ourselves in anything. We can visualize and talk with our loss in our minds' eyes. Religious people can imagine a good place where their lost ones might be.

Alternative solutions for the grief of loss

- Determine a defense mechanism (e.g., denial, minimization, rationalization, etc.).
- Establish forms of expression for your grief.
- Implement rituals that help you bid farewell to the loss.
- Generate alternative diversion activities.
- Identify positive things about your loved one and how those things might be remembered.
- Learn to recognize dependency on the person you lost and refocus on independent life activities.
- Reduce and resolve anger or guilt toward the person you lost and focus on positive recollections.

Dependency

Psychological dependency can be expressed in a very unhealthy way, and it is a serious problem in some families. A psychologically dependent person is capable of taking care of him—or herself, but he or she deeply beliefs that his or her well-being is in the hands of other people. The difference between psychological dependency and the dependency of physically disabled people is that a psychologically healthy person, even one with physical and medical problems, is capable of surviving and functioning with his or her wide range of limits independently from other people.

Psychological dependency includes such forms of negative thinking as low self-esteem, self-criticism, exaggeration, predicting the future, perfectionism, social comparison, expecting approval, fear of rejection, etc., which support dependency and dysfunctional behavior. A dependent person awaits constant instruction and confirmation that gives him or her approval, despite the fact that he or she could do things on his or her own.

Instead of concentrating on his or her own efforts, completing tasks gradually, and paying attention to positive results, this person is so overwhelmed by the idea of being his or her own master and so stupefied by the volume of problems that he or she hesitates to make his or her own choices and decisions. As a result, this person remains inactive without someone else's say-so. This person tends to please everyone, not just who he or she depends upon, in order to be secure in the knowledge that others will take care of him or her when he or she needs or thinks he or she needs help. As result, this person carries out many more tasks and dysfunctional actions than is necessary to get the right help from others. This can also happen when this person remains unaware that situations in life reflect nonconformities and imbalances in interpretations of the basic belief system or basic values, as well as when other people in addition to this person are using negative thinking such as double standards and egocentrism.

The famous writer F. I. Dostoyevsky in his novel *The Village of Stepanchikov* represented a colorful person who manipulated other people's basic belief systems and squeezed his rich friend in a way that was suitable for his own sake and interests, because this rich character suffered from psychological dependency that deceived his own interests.

Alternative solutions for dependency

- Believe in your self-worth and in your own abilities. Identify and clarify social needs.
- Constantly work in the direction of satisfying your own needs by your own efforts in a way that leads to and increases healthy independency.
- Determine the boundaries and limits of healthy dependency.
- Learn how to say no to inappropriate requests.
- Develop assertive and controlled behavior when other people violate the boundaries, which are necessary for establishing healthy independency.
- Allow other people to do things for you without feeling guilt or an obligation to return the gesture.

- Stop taking excessive responsibilities to fulfill difficult loads and favors for other people to the detriment of your own interests.
- Decrease sensitivity to criticism.
- Create balance between healthy dependency and healthy independency.
- Learn to make decisions and follow through with actions to gain your own experience and bolster your confidence.
- Collect more precise data and information to make correct decisions and positive interpretations.
- Accept responsibility for mistakes, that failure is a necessary part of life, and that errors and imperfections are part of human nature, without losing self-confidence and self-esteem.
- Learn to respect and satisfy your own needs as well as the needs of others as much as possible without self-sacrifices.

Alcohol and Drug Addiction

There is no doubt that it is distressing if someone in the family has been associated with alcohol or drug addiction. The treatment of such people is not only vital and essential for them but also for their families. Chemical dependency can lead to serious psychological and physical problems, and also to criminal activities, which can destroy the physical and mental health of the addicted person. Dependency is a chemical imbalance in the human organism that is under the influence of addictive chemical substances; this causes the normal coordinative function of the brain to stall, which reflects disharmony and loss of control over the body.

Some people are predisposed to chemical dependency, which is determined by genetic, familial, and social factors. The inability to resist stress, poor willpower, low self-esteem, depression, anxiety, and panic attacks often accompany conditions of alcohol and drug addiction. In the human organism, the chemical balance of neuro-hormones specifies normal intellectual activity and depends on the reversible reactions of disintegration and production of neurostimulators along with the system of feedback.

This chemical balance of neurohormones includes reversible control over each if it is excessive in quantity. When the amount of one neurohormone exceeds the other, this stimulates an opposite reaction of reduction to its synthesis and strengthened production of ferments, which amplify the disintegration of these neurohormones. Vice versa, the reduction in concentration of necessary neuroactive agents leads to stimulation of the ferments, which amplify the synthesis of neurohormones. In essence, this chemical control is disrupted by the chronic use of addictive substances.

Once this balance has been interfered with by chronic use of drugs and alcohol, the body can't function normally. It displays a variety of very unpleasant and even life-threatening symptoms that prompt an addicted person to take more drugs and alcohol in increased dosages, which can kill a person. In this case, addictive drugs are substitutes for the normal neurohormones of the body. That means the more chemicals an addicted person takes, the more he or she suppresses the production of the body's own chemicals. Then reduced quantities of the addictive agent leads to disruption of human function as a consequence of the suppressed production of the necessary neurohormones, which then tends to support symptoms of physical and psychological dependency.

The addictive chemical agent upon which a person becomes dependent establishes physical and mental control over him or her. It forces that person to obtain the necessary dose of the addictive substance at any cost and by any means in order to reduce his or her unstable balance, which is temporary until the next dose. Chemical dependency affects the functioning of an addicted person with his or her family and community in ways that can be irreversible and dangerous. How do people know about the fateful consequences and about how easy it is to become an addict and still not be afraid to use drugs?

The answer is distrust that this information is the truth, because any information that emanates from experiences of other people can be false. Lies and contradictions in people's adherence to their basic belief systems; inability to exercise precise analysis of facts and events; absence of correct judgment related to error in comparing realistic and positive data; denial of the worth of human existence; pessimism and depression—all this testifies to the tendency of people with these conditions toward spontaneous decomposition and self-destruction.

Alternative solutions to alcohol and drug addiction

- Acknowledge the harmfulness of the consumed chemical substances and alcohol and the possibility of curtailing their control over your body.
- Concentrate on the positive impacts of being off the drugs and sober.
- Establish reasons that cause chemical dependency (e.g., negative thinking, events, patterns of behavior, etc.) and obtain professional help.
- Reexamine the system of basic values that justifies chemical dependence.
- Identify innovative lifestyles and ways of thinking that direct you toward freedom from drugs and alcohol.
- Reduce sensitivity to stress and criticism, and increase self-esteem and self-appraisal.
- Develop the right responses and stability in stressful, unfair, and anger-producing situations that stimulate chemical dependence.
- Stop just promising to change and take action by making gradual changes step-by-step. Take small steps one at a time toward the target of eliminating addiction to drugs and alcohol.
- Identify how chemical dependency can possibly lead to criminal activity and destroy personal and social bonds.
- Attend a twelve-step program to maintain substance and alcohol abuse recovery.
- Increase your involvement in distracting activities, which will divert you toward strengthening your health and restoring your body's functions.

PROBLEMS AT WORK

Pressure at work is a universal problem, the resolution of which becomes essential and vital for most people. Whenever we experience resistance and pressure connected with colleagues' or bosses' requests that are hard to fulfill, it is better to ponder the process of work and the benefit of the job. No less important is strengthening your faith in your own worth and doing the best you can to boost your hope for good luck and success. We achieve success through our best efforts and our ability to overcome difficulties and not fall into pathological mental conditions. We also have a choice to write another resume showcasing our abilities and to develop skills to impress at interviews for a new job.

But for the majority of us, it would be wise and sufficient to improve everyday efforts at our present workplaces and increase our professional qualities without turning our attention to small problems and failures. If we operate according to negative forms of thinking like social comparison, fear of rejection and punishment, and personalization, we can place ourselves behind success. Sensitivity to criticism, low self-esteem, catastrophization, predicting the future, perfectionism, egocentrism, double standards, and personalization also hinder our advances in our occupations. Complaints and unjustified requirements presented when we deserve raises should to be particularly reasonable if we feel strongly about it; otherwise, it can slow deserved advancement and rewards in our careers.

Our bosses and coworkers are also human beings, and they might feel the same ways we do, and in their place we might respond and behave in the same way. By putting ourselves in their shoes, we will correctly not take things personally and will not be offended by coworkers and bosses' behavior toward us in certain circumstances. It might be reasonable not to take the reactions of coworkers and bosses personally because their unfairness or inquiries could be caused by reasons that don't relate to us. If we consider taking responsibility for our own actions and not focusing on the actions of others, in this case we can feel more comfortable at our workplaces.

Alternative solutions to problems at work

- Determine strategies that will establish collaboration and healthy relations with coworkers and authorities.
- Identify your own role in problems at your workplace.
- Replace negative forms of thinking (projection, egocentrism, double standards, personalization, catastrophization, perfectionism, low-self-esteem, social comparison, etc.) with balanced, healthy thinking and display solid but flexible behavior.
- Understand the circumstances that led to the vocational problems.
- Concentrate on your efforts on their elimination and on positive results.
- Review success in all areas of your life, including the workplace, to maintain appropriate self-confidence.
- Accept criticism as valid, consider it, and reverse it. This promotes motivation and success in the future without exaggerating your mistakes or becoming anxious.
- Resolve conflict situations with by employing neutral and respectful communications skills.

FEAR OF BEING CONTROLLED

Problems with fear of being controlled or losing control of situations and other people are a borderline trait of this mental disorder. The negative types of thinking in this mental condition include fear of rejection or abandonment, emptiness, all-or-nothing, egocentrism, blaming, hopelessness, anger, humiliation, jumping to conclusions, using ultimatum words, etc. The other symptom that complicates this problem is an excessive impulse to spend money and shop, engage in multiple sexual conducts, or collect unnecessary things, or enthusiasm in senseless activities—all of which affect a person's normal functioning in society. Being in opposite feelings and states of mind is a manifestation of this kind of problem. This tangled nature and carelessness reflects confusion in the basic belief system and establishes incorrect and unhealthy uses and directions that deceive a person and exert pressure on the people around him or her.

Determining the form of negative thinking, behavior, and underlying beliefs that cause the fear of being controlled is essential to establish balance with other people and the environment. Fear of being controlled and the tendency to establish excessive control over other people are two opposite states in which a person with this disorder engages. Dualism is part of the philosophy of the famous writer

F. I. Dostoyevsky; it reflects two tendencies of the human personality: to be dominative (boss) and to be repressed (slave). Within the standard, normally those tendencies are in balance, but in this condition it is not. In this case, the imbalance interferes with functioning. When a person is in the depressed state, he or she is repressed and engages in self-destructing and self-mutilating thinking and actions. When a person is in the dominative stage, the manifestation of this state is expressed through the desire to establish excessive control over others, including suppression and oppression of the interests of other people. This person's behavior tries to prevent the repressed stage by performing manipulative actions to take this undivided control.

Alternative solutions for the fear of being controlled

- Establish and challenge negative forms of thinking and underlying distorted beliefs that are supporting this problem
- Discover self-worth and "I" messages with a good sense of value that reduce aggression, anger, mutilation, and destructive behavior.
- Learn self-control, assertiveness, and benign explanations of other people's motivations.
- Impede the expression of excessive control over others.
- Learn to be comfortable alone, without the company of people.
- Switch your attention from thoughts of fear of abandonment or rejection to solitary and productive activities that fulfill your needs.
- Reexamine childhood abuse or abandonment in producing psychological problems, and develop balanced acceptance of things that can't be changed.
- Reduce compulsive behavior and activities.
- Recognize others' positive and negative traits and tendencies after establishing correct, unbiased opinions and fair conclusions.
- Learn the negative consequences of too much control and negative judgment of other people.

Panic Attacks

Panic attacks are a condition with which everyone is familiar. Shaking, palpitations, difficulty breathing or shallow breathing, sweating, cold hands and feet, dizziness, nausea, vomiting, redness or pallor of skin, fear of dying, fainting, chest pain, headaches, stomach pain, frequent urges to urinate and defecate at inappropriate times—those are the manifestations of panic disorder. The fear comes from negative thinking of rejection, punishment, guilt, shame, shyness, magnification, catastrophization, predicting bad things, etc. Trauma, accidents, criticism, abuse, and outrage from childhood or adulthood, as well as natural disasters, are triggers for panic attack disorder, which is when the brain can't maintain a stable state and balance with reality.

The resemblance of unthreatening objects or events to past fears and exaggerations can be serious grounds for a panic attack in an unstable mind. Normally we fear specific situations, but after we become familiar with those experiences, our fears cease. We get accustomed to unknown situations by facing them, and after acquainting ourselves with those events, we cease alarm or other discomfort. That is how we overcome our fears.

But what happens if the fear persists and we start to avoid the fearful situation? This sometimes means that the disease called panic disorder is developing, which in addition to psychological symptoms (avoidance of situations and activities that cause disturbances and fear) is accompanied by physical symptoms similar to other medical problems. We learn through life to maintain life stressors using an accessible shielding mechanism. We also learn skills to adapt to stress and fear of some situations and protect ourselves from anything that disrupts our balance in life. When we use this mechanism in irrational and dysfunctional ways, we experience fear and panic attacks, which reflect a series of symptoms and actions in pathological form.

Alternative solutions to panic attacks

- Determine forms of negative thinking and series of supporting beliefs that produce panic attacks.
- Divert your attention toward different distracting and enjoyable activities.
- Identify differences between real threats and imaginable threats.
- Face situations that are only threatening in your imagination.
- Use graded exposure: gradually, step-by-step experience facing your fear in situations and activities that seem threatening and cause panic attacks.
- Focus on positive aspects and use positive imagery to minimize fear.
- Use positive and reality-based interpretations and replacements of negative thoughts.
- Accept errors and oversights as part of the living process.
- Use relaxation exercises and activities.
- Alternately imagine a safe and reliable place and then a situation that causes fear. Notice your intermediate condition between the two states (from excitation to relaxation and vice versa). Be able to imagine this safe place when you experience fear; this is known as desensitization.
- Rehearse every step of facing a forthcoming timid situation in your mind, and imagine a positive outcome in resolution of this condition.
- Concentrate on positive results and success.

ANXIETY

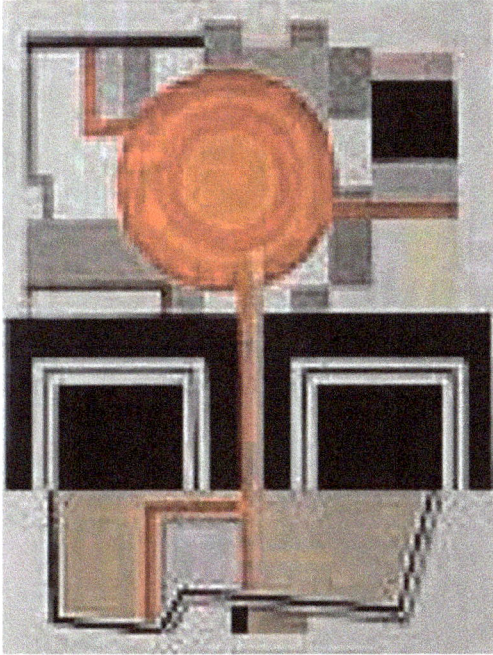

Anxiety appears with the threat of danger or instability in our lives, which also can be manifested in loss of control, going crazy, fear of death, fainting, heart attacks, fatigue, muscle tension, twitching, shaking, restlessness, difficulty breathing, a lump in the throat, palpitations, cold hands and feet, frequent urination, diarrhea, hot flashes or chills, feeling on edge, inability to concentrate, insomnia, and irritability. Anxiety is different from other phobias and panic attacks because of the absence of consistent avoidance behavior (specific actions or situations). Anxiety is the body's natural reaction to stress and other threatening situations. It normally disappears after a little while. In the case of disease, anxiety remains prominent in casual and nonthreatening situations and seriously affects a person's ability to function.

The basis for anxiety and worries are subconscious thoughts and persuasions, which are sometimes impossible to keep in balance with reality. These thoughts and persuasions are produced by underlying dysfunctional and irrational thinking and beliefs. Relieving discomfort and unpleasant feelings related to anxiety is possible with the application of the solution of a problem and abstraction with helpful and necessary relaxation exercises. Other helpful diversion exercises include focusing on neutral things, studying the smallest components and details of surrounding objects (paintings, sculptures, the things around us, etc.), reading, or paying attention to anything that takes our attention away from the irritating thoughts and distracts us from anxiety.

Mainly, reducing the intensity, frequency, and duration of anxiety and tension depends on the revision and reevaluation of our basic and supportive beliefs, which are the main tools in relieving anxiety symptoms. When they take over the control of thought and persuasion, we will then develop the functional and adaptive thinking with positive tendencies in the explanations of existing phenomena. Anxiety and worries will be decreased considerably, or they will completely disappear from your life. Together with changes in thinking and persuasions, it is very important to conduct changes in behavior and actions, which reflect more adequate and normal reactions for manifestations of the environment or internal conflicts. Accommodating our belief systems to discrepancies of other people's belief systems, which also interfere with our lives, is a part of winning control of anxiety symptoms. Generating a behavioral style that is suitable to our present life situations is key in managing anxiety manifestations as well as regulating life stressors.

Alternative solutions for anxiety

- Determine unresolved conflicts in life.
- Recognize encouraging aspects at any given moment of present life situations, and increase selfconfidence and faith in your own success.
- Use positive guided imagery of relaxing situations or situations that cause anxiety. With successive imagination of

relaxing situations, memorize the passage from one state to the other as a coping mechanism.

- Implement stress reduction exercises, thinking, and behavioral patterns.
- According to the rational emotive method, replace irrational thinking and beliefs with positive interpretations and modifications based on reality.
- Reexamine past emotional trauma and anxiety-producing experiences as making no sense or rationality at the present time in order to decrease its value in your life. Decatastrophize, desensitize, and revolve the new vision yourselves as a survivor.
- Implement the paradoxical intervention so that you experience anxiety for a definite period of time in order to decrease the frequency and duration of anxiety and develop a feeling of rational experience without discomfort.
- Concentrate on resolving small and large problems that may reduce troubles and stressors at the present and in the future rather than on feelings of anxiety.
- Develop acceptance of unchangeable facts that were achieved outside our will—no regrets, guilt, predicting the future, fear of punishment, humiliation, self-hate, or self-criticism.
- Focus on the little positive things in the present moment rather than big or small discord in life.

Disorganized Thinking

Disorganized thinking and behavior are main features of schizophrenia. In severe instances, it is expressed in free and senseless speech, and awkward and bizarre behavior, which rigorously affect this person's quality of communication with other people and disturb the functional level of this person to some degree in different aspects of life. But does it reflect different distortions in unobvious forms of normal human affections if this person learns to hide dysfunctional thinking and behavior and becomes perfectly skilled at copying standard phrases and manners that concern meaningless displays of thinking, speech, and behavior? It is a big question and a debatable topic, and it becomes a serious predicament for doctors and psychologists trying to distinguish concealed forms of disease. It may reveal itself only once or only in one aspect; at all other times the person's disorganized thinking and behavior goes unnoticed and doesn't affect general functioning in his or her community.

It seems that people with unremarkable signs in expression of disorganized thinking in their speech and behavior can be extraordinary in many areas of life. They can be sufficiently productive in different areas of science, arts, technology, etc., but in political and economical spheres, they can't be efficient without strong opposition and debate with other people who have more organized and appropriate thinking and behavior based on the main system of values and true point of views. The world knows examples of productive people with mental disorders like F.I. Dostoyevsky; Van Gough; Byron; the mathematical genius John Nash, who inspired the book and film *A Beautiful Mind,* and others. It is undoubted that mental disorders do not affect all aspects of a functional mind. Rather they demonstrate the amazing fact of genius in the human intellect when there is some distortion in thinking and behavior.

Alternative solutions to disorganized thinking

- Identify distortion in thinking, speech, and behavior.
- Make a clear distinction between distortions and normal thinking and why distortions are not efficient.
- Accept the fact that some distortions in thinking and behavior unimportantly and unremarkably disrupt with minimum impact your own and other people's lives.
- Use role-playing, simulations, and modeling to develop proper communication skills in society.
- Recognize limitations and circumstances that are not controlled enough and can't be removed or improved in thinking and behavior at some stage.
- Reduce the influence of stress from unsolved past life conflicts and problems by resolving them with the help of a supportive group of people.
- Determine the most general and vigorous human qualities and features that associate your personality with other healthy people, besides mental problems.
- Strengthen feelings of dignity and self-worth by directing maximum effort to achieving vital tasks with help and mobilization of your own means and assistance of a supportive group (friends, community, and family).

PARANOID DELUSIONS

Paranoid delusions are a group of distortions in thinking and behavior that represent a person's inability to have realistic, positive, and rational explanations of other people's intentions. As a result, based on delusional beliefs, the person suspects that people intend to cause him or her harm. These suspicions may appear in direct statements and accusations of innocent people of intentions of murder, poisoning, injury, torment, etc.—all as a result of illusions, morbid imagination, and exaggeration of danger while the full integrity and safety of this person remains intact. Paranoid ideas sometimes represent forms of errors as a result of deficiency in precise information or unconsidered assumptions that unfortunately exist among a healthy population with detrimental interpretations of basic human values; meanwhile, those people can be mixed with paranoid delusional patients. Sometimes suspicious ideas present in healthy people, who are able to make inferences from a small number of facts to reach the right conclusions.

All of this reflects the difficulty in diagnosing paranoid delusion. The symptoms of paranoid delusion correspond with fear, obsessions, and inability to have normal function, which disarrange the life of a delusional person. Paranoid thinking is based on negative thinking that includes mixing thought with fact, predicting the future, mental filtering, overgeneralization, catastrophization, fear of rejection or punishment, and projection.

As in the case of deceptive thinking in patients who have a negative concentration and focus under the influence of stress on negative aspects and pessimistic interpretations, for delusional people errors and misconceptions oftentimes cause distortions and errors in distinguishing real facts from delusional thinking. This causes delusions and paranoia to occur as symptoms of severe depression. The differentiation between realistic and imaginable situations underlies the basic task of psychological correction and treatment of paranoid delusion and similar states by the method of modifying thinking and behavior.

Collection of accurate information, constant testing, experience, and new facts with an objective and positive focus on real facts help treat paranoid patients and serve as essential keys to decrease or eliminate paranoid ideas and delusions. Patients with paranoid delusion need treatment with medications and psychological intervention such as modification of thinking and behavior and supportive therapy. Healthy people with paranoid convictions could benefit from antidepressants and light, calming of the nervous system medication.

Alternative solutions to paranoid delusions

- Learn to distinguish real, trustworthy facts from errors in thinking and constructing social relations.
- Develop strategies based on calm, thoughtful, and peaceful assumptions and nonaggressive, deliberate actions in relations with other people.
- Define the inadequacy and inaccuracy in thinking and actions that led to your difficulties in contact with other

people and, as a consequence, to you facilitating and supporting paranoid delusion.

- Eliminate the possibility of projecting your own anger in a developing delusion as a basis of mistrust toward others in the absence of self-confidence and the occurrence of excessive apprehensive thinking and unreasonable behavior.
- Determine negative ways of thinking and replace distorted cognitions with positive, nonthreatening interpretations that correspond to reality by applying modification of thinking and behavior concepts.
- Take medications prescribed by the doctor.
- Concentrate on precise and checked facts when constructing relations with others.
- Reexamine ideology and the persuasion of the basic and supportive belief system, which support paranoid ideas and delusions.
- Apply role-playing and modeling as a method in the improvement of communication with others to reduce stress in social interactions.
- Refocus your life on resolving present problems and meeting your own needs.
- In your search for proof, in case of its absence, avoid being quick to lay unjustified blame and accusations. Instead, use trustful and flexible tactics that correspond to reality, and accept the lack of information in a benign way that excludes or reduces conflicts and problems that are connected with your own paranoid ideas.
- Make a cost-benefit analysis for specific fears, and identify the irrational basis for them by investigating the pros and cons. Then use percentages and mathematical estimations to construct correct thinking and behavior.
- Maintain life relationships and focus on the positive aspects of your achievements.

AVOIDANCE

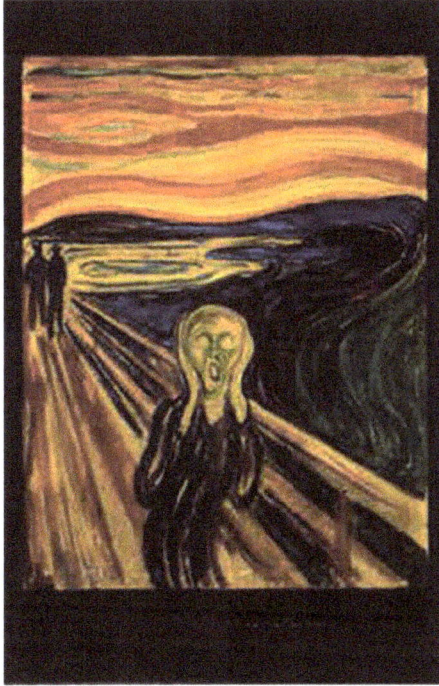

Avoidance of people, situations, and actions are frequently appearing problems that trap people with avoidance into a system of irrational thinking and behavior. Avoidance includes many types of negative thinking: personalization, exaggeration, minimization, projection, self-criticism, low self-esteem, blaming self, jumping to conclusions, thinking of rejection, fear of punishment, expecting approval, mistaking identity, social comparison, guilt, shame, shyness, predicting the future, etc.

Certainly the person who suffers avoidance has a distortion in the basic belief system, and those associated views and persuasions lead to dysfunctional thinking and behavior, exaggeration, and misrepresentation of events and facts that support this problem. Thoughts of possible errors, disappointments in one's own abilities, and probable consequences of failure are exaggerated by this person's mind and lead to avoidance of actions, events, and people instead of curiosity to do something and watch what happens.

It is necessary to make certain efforts in order to overcome avoidance. One must adapt to inertia in actions and overcome fear with complex pathological thinking and patterns of behavior by the gradual exposure technique. Other helpful efforts include beneficial recognition of this problem, changes in persuasions and interpretations of underlying beliefs that feed negative ways of thinking; replacement with positive, realistic, precise data; and consideration to avoid jumping to conclusions. Reevaluation of dysfunctional avoidant behavior is a clue in assuring a new type of more adaptive and functional patterns of behavior instead of maladaptive old schemas. Encouraging efforts and results should be rewarded immediately. Modification of thinking and behavior don't show enough value without introducing the new elements that reflect adequate thinking and behavior.

Alternative solutions to avoidance

- Decrease fear of rejection while increasing your sense of self-worth and self-acceptance.
- Learn to satisfy your own most necessary needs. Form realistic purposes and tasks that correspond to real possibilities and are commensurate with your capacity.
- Learn to praise the value of your achievements without exaggeration by exercising positive selftalk to improve self-esteem and self-confidence.
- Develop assertive and functional communication skills: praise others; accept compliments from others; manifest sympathy, understanding, and sincerity in appropriate situations; know how to politely decline unreasonable requests that require excessive effort from you; listen more rather than talk; reduce small details in when talking about yourself; consider the interests of other people; direct conversation to neutral topics that are pleasant for other people and don't excite resistance and irritation that might concern

them; be flexible and cooperative, not rigid; laugh more and tell jokes in appropriate moments without contempt and mockery; don't insist on your opinions and persuasions, but show your opinion in a solid way without disrespect; don't be inhibited to present your needs; learn to accept the same from others; hold balance as far as possible between your interests and the interests of others; compromise and reestablish previously wrong impressions of others.

- Concentrate on positive emotions and events in contact with other people; learn to predict positive experiences and sketch in your imagination realistic iridescent pictures of expected encounters and good situations.
- Forego devaluing and discounting positive data about yourself and others.

ISOLATION

Social isolation reflects the incapacity of a personality to associate according to the standards of society as a consequence of mental or medical problems. It also reveals an imbalance in following basic values by the isolated person and other people in the community. This displays different contradictory abutments and brings isolation to individuals or a group of people in a specific society.

Places that can increase the chances of social contacts and social interactions have limitations also, and it depends on the social status of the different groups of people in society at the present moment. The possibilities of using even normal social skills in the social contacts also have limitations because of the stratifications, conditionality, and structure of society, which frequently represent the basic systems of views and values in a specific period of time.

Successful people and people who are far from success (e.g., mental patients and people with other kinds of disabilities) can be lonely and deprived of normal contact with other people; they usually avoid social contact for many reasons. The more frequent reason for social isolation appears for a specific type of personality and people with mental disorders, who specifically avoid contact with other people. The isolation, which is expressed by feelings of loneliness and discomfort among people, frequently reflects the conditions of people with physical disabilities.

Along with this, a society and its system of beliefs and values can also cause barriers to communication for some perfectly healthy individuals who, for one reason or another, do not comply with the rules established by the society and refuse to play the roles dictated by circumstances in that society.

In this case, people who refuse to pretend and play multiple games in appropriate ways or who defend their own personalities from confusion and harm by all kind of pretending in their community feel rejected and become isolated, uncomfortable, unhappy, and disappointed. The main strategy in such cases is to learn recognition of one's own worth and value as a human being, contribute to social development, reestablish one's perception of his or her and other people's consciousness in self-significance, be in balance to obtain and return, be grateful, and request gratification from others in undeviating or tortuous ways as necessary.

It is also necessary to understand the limitation of this balance, which depends on the reasonable basis of those requests and the ability to accept some determinations of discordance in fortune and luck for a successful social life. Negative forms of thinking like fear of rejection or expecting approval do not promote social adequacy; on the contrary, they endorse loneliness and desperation, isolation and disappointment.

Differences in the merits and abilities of financial and social freedom are not such inevitable facts for successful social involvement. Success has been achieved in business relations and commercial areas by way of improved knowledge of the nature of human relations and the best communication abilities in different groups of people. The success and prosperity of different people and groups in society have seriously been determined by the development of specific strategies and attention to each individual personality in society. Those strategies strictly consider a person's own interest in combination with the interests of other people, which can satisfy 60 percent or more in the realization of basic human values.

An increase in deviation in some circumstances, and possibilities to return to the basic principles, both in balance with a person's own integrity and interests are necessary to function successfully in society. It is an art that includes dynamic changes from conventional forms and pretending in social roles and games that have been established by present society. Preservation of one's own and other people's interests as a whole—bearing in mind the changes, progress, and compromise in the installation and interpretations of basic human views in each period of time, with an internal review and assessment of the eligibility of any derogation—is a key strategy in the success of communication.

No less important in socializing is luck: properly made efforts that take into account the limitation of action and the circumstances of driving forward in balance with the needs, along with the direction of fate and requirements of society.

Many books and other sources of literature are devoted to this subject. Dale Carnegie wrote numerous books about appropriate and comfortable communication. A lot of people have learned to pretend feelings and conditions they do not really experience at the moment, and they have developed the complex games with wearing different masks for successful communication at the social level. Frequently these pretentions in society do not imply internal balance with the system of basic values, which has supported human society for thousands of years. As a result, some people might feel disappointed in the skillful communications of people who are pretending, which conquered their hearts. In summation, the majority of people expect the full values of the implied symbols. Delusiveness and disappointments in public relations in conflict with the rules of simple human politeness are expressed both in correspondence and nonconformity with the principles and laws of basic human values.

As has already been emphasized repeatedly, the absence of balance in the world strongly slants the overall possibility of avoiding the full value of all existing rules and laws, which allow us to establish necessary flexible control and take into account all existing circumstances and changes in society.

Revision of inoperative installations, which prevent contradictions between principles, commensuration of priorities, and the necessary limited and substantiated compromises without disturbance of the order of society or laws of the state, is also a condition for successful socializing.

Public functioning includes the difference between pretending or being just polite, which with time will show how misleading people can be, and concentrating on real positive aspects. Pardoning and restoring disrupted connections are important components also, as well as being extremely understandable, flexible, cooperative, and diplomatic; having an idea how the same reality works for us and others; and explaining other people's intentions by using realistic visions of our own interests and the interests of others.

In other words, we need to see expressing politeness and pretention as being as different as truth and unrealistic meanings of human contact. This is necessary so that we may pass through our emotions and possible reactions and put ourselves in the places of other people in similar conditions. Only then we can understand, explain, and forgive other people without being stuck in the egocentrism (negative thinking) that complicates our communication. It is no less important not to be struck by other forms of negative thinking besides the egocentrism, such as unhealthy forms of social comparison, mistaken identity, labeling, exaggeration, jumping to conclusion, etc.

As a result of these forms of negative thinking, isolation is a choice for the person as a consequence of dysfunctional and illogical thinking. In spite of the unsteady social position or mental disorder, such people must begin from the very first step: reconstructing their relationship with themselves; increasing self-esteem and self-appraisal; stopping expectations of approval, conformation, and praise from others; quitting unjustified self-condemnations, self-criticism, self-hatred, and self-humiliation; following the simple diagram presented in the beginning of this book; and gradually increasing their faith and conviction in this method's power and their own worth and rightness.

The second step is to learn and use appropriate communication skills based on knowledge of how other people (or themselves) would like to be treated in different life situations. They must also allow themselves to make mistakes, come up short, and pretend, while at the same time forgiving themselves and others. This will help them practice and develop habits for smooth and comfortable socializing in any community without hypocrisy, negative thinking, or inappropriate behavior. Instead they will express respect, cooperation, and love for other people.

The wrong choices are learning love only for themselves, exercising in double standard negative thinking, and placing their interests over others'. If they do these things, the disharmony and imbalance in society will be greater than before. Historically, one group of people made their rights a special, exclusive priority, and other groups of people didn't know or even try to seriously take control, set priorities for their own rights, or realize those rights in realistic and healthy ways. However, the use of positive, realistic thinking based on a strong system views and persuasions can be a good promoter of healthy and comfortable contacts between people in society without unreasonable pretending or self-defeating features.

Alternative solutions to isolation

- Identify negative ways of thinking such as fear of rejection, shame and shyness, social comparison, double standards, jumping to conclusions, exaggeration, egocentric thinking, mistaken identity, and fakery that are based on your childhood and negative experiences in socializing.
- Concentrate on previous positive experiences and use prior successful social skills.
- Persistently initiate social contacts and interactions; focus on your efforts and pleasant experiences.

- Recognize advantages and disadvantages, which reflect the same qualities, in the ways you are like other people, and assert equality with them.
- Set reasonable boundaries and limitations in social contacts and interactions, and notify other people about your intentions in peaceful and calm ways.
- Learn the skill of conducting pleasant conversations, taking into account each individual's needs with a specific approach and posing positive questions that correspond to the Socratic method.
- Gain trust and confidence in your own social abilities. Accept imperfections and limitations of you and other people.
- Follow conventional communication skills: listen more than speak; ask positive questions; refocus an argumentative or irritating object of conversation to a neutral and pleasant theme of conversation; honor others with worthy praise and assume with appreciation compliments given to you; be sincere by using social comparison in a healthy manner and healthy estimation; keep in mind the value of all interpretations of your words and how this will return to you; know how to move away flexibly from strict rules and conditionality if this corresponds to general human values and views; be responsible for your own behavior; pardon your errors and the errors of other people, taking into account exceptions to the rules and new circumstances that led to them; don't assume everyone is absolutely perfect; be prepared for any outcome in communication; don't take everything personally or expect the impossible from others by making valid estimations about other people; be self-sufficient, variable, independent, and skillful in accomplishing tasks and purposes, as well as assertive in a healthy and realistic way.

Delusional Ideas

Delusion is one kind of problem that is related to negative ways of thinking like mixing thought with fact; jumping to conclusions; exaggeration; predicting the future, etc. A delusion can be presented in the form of an unrealistic idea that contradicts obvious facts in many aspects of thinking and behavior. The paranoid delusion was discussed earlier in this book.

Other examples of a delusional idea can involve predicting desirable success or disaster on the basis of unjustified and contradicting scientific facts, or even based on pseudoscientific predictions that use incorrect theory, poor research, and unfinished work with experimental studies. If these ideas include untested facts and are reinforced by false theory, then a person suffering from delusion can fall into serious error, passing from delusion to insanity in the true sense of the word, and with the entire range of consequences. Delusion can seriously change a person's behavior and take it in the incorrect direction with the development of a psychosis that severely affects how he or she functions in his or her community.

Sometimes delusions can be so obvious in a conversation that the close contact and manners of behavior of the delusional person quickly come to the attention of other people. But in some cases these ideas can be obscured and shaded by a realistic and seemingly trustworthy wrapper that can represent a normal manner and form; only wrong and troubled results might indicate delusional aspects of this person's thinking. In all instances, it is possible to avoid or ease pathological manifestations in delusional thinking and behavior if we collect precise data and compare it with scientific facts and our own and other people's experiences and observations. This would help free us from delusional and distorted thinking and behavior. Undoubtedly, error and distortion in any person's thinking and con- clusions might reflect a lack of information, knowledge, and theory in this period of time, which can inflict untrue delusional ideas and dysfunctional behavior.

If delusional thinking and behavior are actively represented and seriously inflicted on a person and a community, then it is possi- ble to assume a mental shift to delusion, which requires professional interference and help. The changed interpretations of basic beliefs and views also induce delusional and distorted thinking, as well as irrational behavior, which is hard to identify and differentiate.

Alternative solutions to delusional ideas

- Gain insight into possibilities of negative and distorted thinking in order to prevent delusional interpretations and confusions.
- Compare your thinking with other people's perspectives and points of view.
- Use verified, scientific, and adjusted data to construct functional thinking.
- Reevaluate your belief system with respect to the beliefs, thinking, and behaviors of other people; determine a more

functional strategy and direction in the prediction of events and situations.

- Acknowledge the possibility of errors and inaccuracies in your thinking, strategies, and behavior.
- Build a more flexible line of behavior and possible retreats from incorrect thoughts in order to control distortion in thinking and behavior.
- Take the professional advice of a doctor or a psychologist if your own analysis of your thinking is either dysfunctional or impossible.
- Take medications as prescribed by a psychiatrist.
- Control all possibilities of inaccurate delusional thinking or the appearance of doubtful ideas as to how they can lead to consequences.
- Don't require anyone to follow or act according to your doubtful ideas until you obtain precise proof of the assumed situations.
- Learn to distinguish reality from imagination and delusion.

DEPRESSION

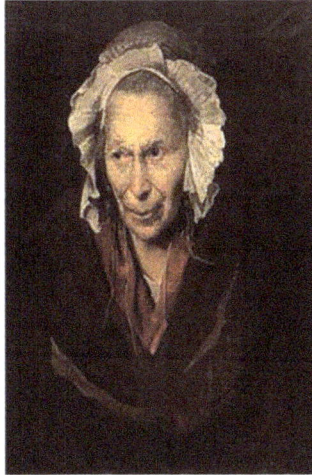

Depression is a common condition that is familiar to everyone who has experienced it at least once in life, even if it was only for a short period of time. But if this condition lasts too long and exceeds more than six months with enough intensity, it becomes a major depressive disorder. This condition reflects a serious imbalance of neurohormones and requires correction and use of medication along with psychotherapy. The psychotherapy is assigned to identify negative and distorted forms of thinking that affect the mood and, as a result, the functioning.

Depression is perceived in very unpleasant feelings that include different types of mental suffering that most people can't see or imagine, despite the indescribable pain a person suffers. However, those feelings have complete control over our brains, and our brains control the feelings that define the concepts of challenging dysfunctional and irrational thinking and behavior in order to reduce or eliminate symptoms of depression. Depression can be a sign of reaction to stress and a complicated life situation and normally disappears when the situation is resolved. But in the case that the depression continues, it impinges on normal life and testifies to the disease.

The famous writer F. M. Dostoyevsky defined depression as punishment; a possibility through the experience of one's own pain to be compassionate and to comprehend the suffering of other people; purity of thinking as well as feeling; and the elimination of all sins and errors, which reflects the cleanliness of religious persuasions and beliefs in a fair way. Since S. Freud and other psychoanalysts declined the role of religious belief in the psychodynamic of any person, those definitions of depression and its course are not topics of modern psychotherapy.

However, as was mentioned earlier, all structure of present society reflects the echoes of religious persuasions, which in turn influence the psychological world of humans, with or without a religious nature to basic views and values. The conflict in a person's belief system, which originated from his or her childhood education under the training of family and society, as well as from distortions in perceptions of real-life situations, causes depression symptoms.

Therefore the need for reevaluation of that belief system and replacement of negative, distorted, and irrational thinking as well as inappropriate behavior in order to treat depression logically emerges. Many years of experience in modifying thinking and behavior has proven the possibility of reducing or eliminating depression symptoms, both with medicines or without them. The numerous forms of negative thinking that were presented earlier can serve as sources of depression and therefore require corrections in addition to revision of the dysfunctional or distorted belief system. Despite the fact of the success of treatment and the methods of modification of thinking and behavior, it is difficult to determine the roots of the dysfunctional persuasions and views that facilitate depressive thinking and irrational behavior. Depression is a symptom in numerous other mental conditions.

The treatment of depression can be a basic part of therapy for many other mental disorders that cannot be corrected without treating the depression first. Depression can promote, complicate, and support resistance in the treatment of many other mental problems. Sometimes treating depression can be very beneficial in the treatment of other mental conditions. Psychological pain can be measurable or not; it depends on each individual's ability to use defense mechanisms in ways that lead to different types of reactions and intensities of depression symptoms, although the intensity of psychological pain depends on the disturbance in the thinking and behavior of a depressive patient.

However, practical psychiatry has developed different forms of measurement that indicate manifestations, intensity, character, capability for recovery, or development of complications. Together with pain and suffering, depression disturbs concentration, memory, and the ability to carry out everyday tasks, and it distorts conclusions as well as behavior. This is at the center of therapy for intense and neglected depression. In cases of extreme hopelessness, ideas and attempts at suicide occur, some with fatal outcomes, which indicates the danger of depression when combined with other mental illnesses that can lead to death.

Alternative solutions for depression

- Identify sources and triggers of depression.
- Reduce the value of sources and triggers to lessen the probability of the onset of depression as much as possible.
- Define negative ways of thinking and underlying dysfunctional, irrational beliefs and their supporting persuasions.
- Replace or modify dysfunctional beliefs and thoughts with positive, realistic persuasions and conclusions, which will lower stress and irrational thinking and behavior.
- Reconcile with losses, errors, and events that cannot be changed and are not in your power to control.
- Learn to use appropriate thinking and adaptive behavior with positive meanings and directions under any circumstances.
- Concentrate on attempts and efforts more than on results, and attach great significance to positive outcomes.
- Establish solid and effective lines of behavior within the framework of reasonable politeness with people who impose unjustified requirements.

- Understand your own and other people's limitations in following general human rules and the system of basic values.
- Obtain prolonged and deep sleep.
- Follow a healthy diet and lifestyle.
- Improve personal hygiene and grooming.
- Use conflict resolution skills to state issues that relate to standing by personal interests and meeting your own needs.
- Resolve interpersonal conflicts.
- Build a support system among your family and community by increasing social bonds and healthy contacts.
- Develop positive self-talk, self-statements, self-descriptions, and self-appraisal based on real facts and qualities that indicate advantageous comparisons and those that increase self-confidence.
- Implement positive, functional schemas of thinking and patterns of behavior that ensure success and contentment with life.
- Concentrate on positive aspects of your present life situation and resolve problems step-by-step by focusing on efforts and positive results.
- Choose more benign and optimistic ways of thinking instead of suicidal thoughts and thoughts of nonexistence that lead to suicidal thinking and behavior.
- Collect more optimistic and precise data in interpretations and conclusions, without concentrating on the negative aspects of life.
- Use stress reduction behavior and appropriate communication to reduce stress and disputes in social contact with other people.
- Laugh and joke more, and increase physical exercise and enjoyable activities, including pleasant social interactions, to increase psychological energy and obtain the feeling of satisfaction and well-being.
- At first, include activities that can potentially bring pleasure, even if it seems unlikely. Predict enjoyment with a positive imagination.

WEIGHT PROBLEMS

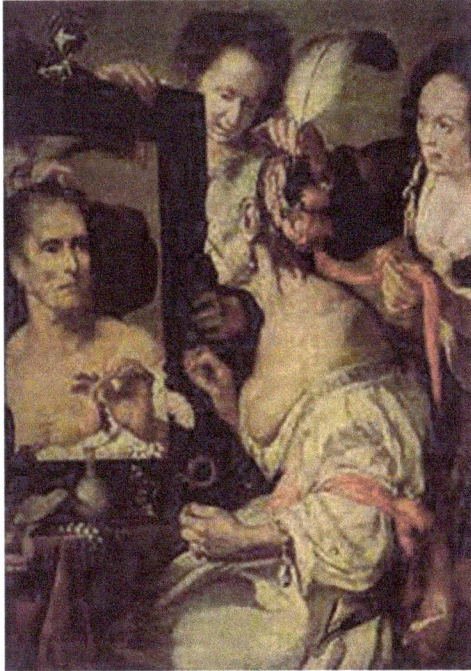

Currently, two opposite conditions connected with concerning weight behavior are a huge problem at the present time. In developed countries, hunger is a small problem, while obesity and overeating remains a big challenge for many people. Another problem connected with weight issues that can lead to health complications is the drastic decrease in weight related to anorexia nervosa. Some types of obesity scientists associate with starvation and/or a lack of proper nutrition in pregnant women; scientists believe this leads to the activation of genes and agents that increase children's need for food and eventually leads to obesity in adulthood.

Some researchers have also revealed data that testifies to the absence of some genes that are critical for the production of indicators that control the level of blood sugar, which is responsible for constant hunger. As a consequence, this leads to eating disorders and obesity. Obesity can also lead to disturbances in the function of the thyroid, adrenal glands, pancreas, gonads, pituitary gland, and other metabolic disorders that are not related to increased food consumption. Other reasons for being overweight include depression, stress, an unhealthy lifestyle that includes eating junk food and fatty food, a lack of physical activity or exercise, some medications, and poor self-control in eating habits. The mental states associated with malnutrition, bulimia, and anorexia nervosa are concerns of psychologists and psychiatrists, who treat patients alongside other doctors.

Another condition that has recently drawn the attention of communities is being underweight, since underweight people (mostly women) can become seriously ill, which can sometimes lead to death. All weight conditions, but mainly bulimia nervosa and anorexia nervosa, are not dependent upon medical conditions; instead they are caused by psychological problems, which are treated by psychologists and other doctors. Such people frequently suffer from depression, low self-esteem, shyness, social discomfort, anxiety, obsessive behavior, poor self-control, fear of rejection, self-criticism, etc.

The establishment of a healthy diet and a healthy lifestyle are difficult to employ because of the strong influence of habits that have been acquired since childhood. Gradually changing unhealthy habits step-by-step and concentrating on efforts can be very efficient in reducing psychological problems in the course of treating disorders connected with weight. Reduction in the size of food portions, exercise, a healthy lifestyle, an increase of physical activity, and enjoyment of different interests and hobbies together with the replacement of negative thinking and a more functional and reevaluated system of views might be key for weight problems.

Alternative solutions to weight problems

- Accept the fact that the problem with weight is not related to the beautiful, developed personality that represents you.
- Acknowledge your own dignity and pride for the way you look at the present time.

- Analyze reasons for possible disturbances of weight (medical, genetic, lifestyle, ways of negative thinking, and irrational beliefs, etc.).
- Develop a positive self-image and vision of yourself with an increase of self-confidence, a constant and simultaneous reduction of irrational self-criticism, and an increase in awareness of your self-worth.
- Use positive self-talk and self-descriptions to improve self-esteem.
- Constantly and gradually change harmful habits that lead to problems with weight.

SEXUAL PROBLEMS

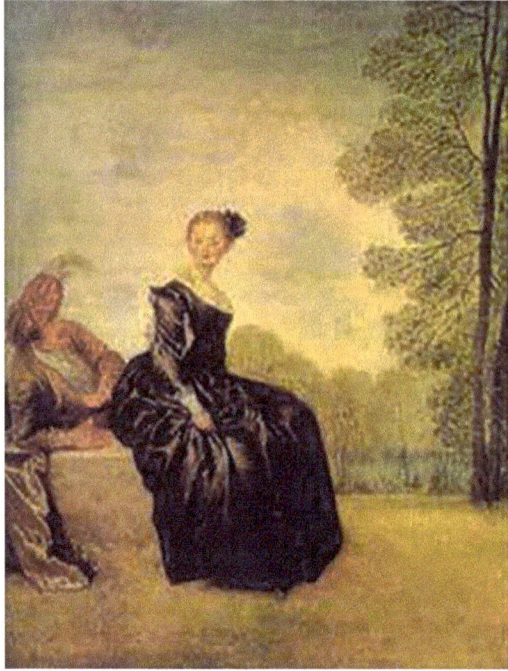

Sexual problems are based on nonconforming sexual motivations in the behavior of men and women that reflect disharmony in the world and stipulate differences in dysfunctions in this area of psychological problems.

The male part of the human population is more strongly subject to sexual inclination, and their behavior is more active and goal directed in obtaining sexual enjoyment with a larger number of sexual partners. They are sometimes implicated in other various forms of sexual satisfaction that are permitted to some degree in society. Male sexual psychological motivations in behavior are determined by genetic and physiological factors. This defines several psychological functions, but the more precise function is to perform the largest possible number of inseminations to ensure survival in the late periods of their lives. The goal is to have children to ensure undivided female attention and the care of at least one woman. This also includes other emerging psychological tasks such as the correspondence and adequacy of social roles and status; obtaining enjoyment from sex and relations, including partnership and friendship with the opposite sex partner; financial responsibility in sexual activities; and also obeying religious limitations and the rules of the community.

Female libido and sexual behavior are also determined by several genetic and psychological tendencies: to have a strong partner with whom it is possible to raise children and who can provide social and financial stability and security for her and her kids; to observe religious and other rules of society; to experience pleasure in sex and be under male attention that reflects involvement in the pleasurable activities that have been established and limited by social rules and community structure.

Freud and his followers have isolated the sexual motivations in thinking and behavior of men and women that, in spite of all desires of idealists, revolutionarily changed our vision of the psychological world of the human race. They proved that suppression of sexual function in some instances plays a role in the origins of disturbances in psychological and other functions of humans. However, this theory has diverted attention from the regulation and guidance of religious institutions in all aspects of human life.

Biological, physiological, and psychological tendencies that have genetic origins have been defined as essential needs, without the roles of religious limitations and guidance, which worked through millennia and built societies for thousands of years. If this religious motivation can be added to Freud's definition of sexual motivation of psychological tendencies, then the meaning of sexual function (as well as dysfunctions of males and females) can be defined and understood more clearly. The reasonable limitations, based on correct interpretations of religious beliefs and rules, allow us to regulate the specific level of meaning in sexual functioning. Today, marriage is still the best solution for sexual relationships; however, religious guidance and genetic predispositions can lead to advantages and disadvantages at the same time.

Awareness and regulation of all tendencies can more harmoniously improve the sexual lives and reproduction functions of humanity in the development of harmonious personalities that define the purpose of large numbers of psychologists and people who seek the solution to psychological dysfunctions. It is possible to consider the homosexual relationship as a different form of the existing and prevailing form of sexuality. Homosexuality might be reexamined as the genetic and psychological deviation accepted by American psychiatric science as a version of the standard. This is concordant to a certain degree with the laws of survival and the establishment of sexual relationships, friendships, and love between homosexual partners; this is impossible for some people in heterosexual partnerships. Homosexual partners also have satisfaction and joy in sex. However, that continues to increase disharmony and sexual problems in society. As defined in previous chapters about the relativity of norms and standards in the mental function of people, we can identify the connection or the nonconformity in sexual deviations and tendencies (in particular, homosexuality) that reflect some kind of experiment in modern society.

Public opinion in many countries sometimes quietly and tolerantly relates to this fashionable flow in sexual orientation, but it is not established sufficiently and clearly enough to be a normal manifestation in social relations on all points. So, the main sexual problems in this section of the book will be discussed as traditional heterosexual problems.

It is evident that sex promotes reproduction and normal functioning in society; the tendency toward the multiplication of the human race and establishment of social status undeniably serves as the background for sexual relations. But still a question remains without a clear answer: how do normal and appropriate forms of sexual relations correspond to the functioning of any society? It is an obvious fact that sex that is not connected with the reproduction of the population is not a stumbling block or an encouragement on a state scale. At the same time, sex justifies healthy partnerships, enjoyment in life, and motivation to progress. Because of this, it plays a significant and prominent role in the development of humanity, and can also be a sensible and inspiring factor in society.

Religious rules and limitations are intended to reduce dishar-mony in sexual relations and seemingly serve as some kind of guid-ance in the labyrinth of the vital struggle for existence. They were essential for the regulation of sexual orientation and sex's involvement in society. Accordingly, some instances of sexual relationships that do not follow usual standards can be acceptable and understood in soci-ety, though they are not encouraged to a larger extent. Disharmony in physical attractions and performances are different when it comes to men and women, and this creates a variety of psychological prob-lems. These differences are defined, as was already mentioned, in the sensation of comfort between sexual partners; in other words, sexu-ally arousing stimuli need to be harmoniously concordant in order for both sexes to gain satisfaction. Along with preparedness for sex, the ability to stay aroused enough before and during sex also remains important. Partners' awareness of disharmony in arousal time and intensity during sexual performance might be essential to treat sexual dysfunctions.

Besides physical problems, psychological problems remain the leading cause of sexual dysfunction. The problems of both sexes dis-play sexual disharmony between physical and psychological needs that severely affect the sex lives of different couples. Being comfort-able together most of the time and being inspired and secure are the main psychological factors in the endorsement of sexual attraction; these factors are based on essential genetically defined instincts of selection and survival. Humanity has learned to improve and sub-stitute the missing components in the expression of genetic features, which interfere with sexual attraction. This can explain complex, and even dangerous, activities such as cosmetic surgery, makeup, mod-ern clothes, and sexual behavior including games, pretending, fakery, flirtation, seduction, and genuine expression of feelings and desires. As long as sexual inclinations are basic mechanisms in the intimate relationships of humans, any means for achieving the objective are in play, including the games pointed out above, for the establishment of long-term and functional bonds like marriage and matrimony.

Most important is the true expression of sexual attraction, and it doesn't matter what kind of sexual behavior a person chooses, whether it's pretending, games, etc. However, marriages and relationships are not based on truthful feelings, which are not based on biological inclinations of sexual relations. Sexual attraction will last until the need for pretending is over. It lasts for so long that it stops the true motives of the relationship that are not connected with the serious driving factors (biological and emotional prerequisites). Most couples unconsciously explain this as an absence of inclination and love.

The psychological and biological expressions of sexual inclinations don't have harmonious prolonged form. In addition, sexual attraction is the most encouraging for psychological attraction; it deepens and enhances personal relationships. The male population is more inclined to cheat and search for new partners than the female population; therefore, it is essential to repress sexual behavior in some situations for men. This reflects religious limitations in sexual relationships, which mostly oppress female seductions in one way or another.

Those limitations remain necessary to avoid sexually transmitted diseases, which include some forms of virus-originated cancerous disease, hepatitis, slow-developing fatal diseases such as AIDS, and other infections. With the generation and application of antibiotics, the threat of bacterial venereal infections has weakened, but this does not protect against diseases of viral origin that are contracted when people engage in unprotected sex without condoms.

As was already said, differences in the physical and psychological needs of both sexes lead to disharmony among couples from time to time. Comfort, inspiration, and qualitative time together is the best way to reinforce sexual attraction and the strengthening of family. This is because of our genetic predispositions toward survival, sexual preferences, and selection inclinations. Successful and functional relationships among couples are related to the presence or absence of children; however, instances of divorce with children might be exceptions.

Limitations in sexual activity without the commitment to marriage are necessary to develop constructive and healthy relations in families. This is important for averting undesirable pregnancies, which lead to psychological problems as a result of defective conditions for the development of children. Raising children in a healthy way needs both parents' efforts, as well as the secure psychological and physical health of the children. This is essential in developing a society with certain stability and values. The strength of family communication and the sexual relationship between spouses, with or without children, according to sexual preferences might improve vital principles in the biological survival and selection tendencies. The preservation of the system of values in sexual activity is necessary for the reliable development of society and successive generations. This is what makes it possible to actualize humans' basic biological and psychological tendencies in different periods of time and in different countries. It also incarnates the fundamental principle of reproduction to new generations.

Separation of sexual behavior from reproductive purpose became a main issue in modern society. However, religious limitations continue to be effective, as was described earlier, in the form of unconscious behavior in following basic human principles and values based on the religious belief systems of different groups of people. Marriage remains the major form of healthy realization of sexual relations and behavior. Under the guidance of central human values, which are expressed in the essential human laws in the manifestation of sexual behavior, other forms of sexual expression can be produced. Frequently, sexual relations without marriage are justified in different forms that are based on the deep human feelings of love, dignity, passion, creative exploration, heroism, etc., and can be admirable in many examples in the arts, literature, movies, theater, and more.

Alternative solutions to sexual problems

- Identify the positive explanations of the events, phenomena, and activities of you and your partner, including conflicts, disagreements, and contradictions in your present relationship.
- Determine your sexual desires and how to possibly fulfill those sexual needs in your relationship with your partner.

- Learn to be open and to share secret desires with your partner.
- Accept some limitations and new possibilities for meeting your sexual needs.
- Identify the psychological basis for problems in your sexual relationship.
- Determine psychological images that reflect your childhood education of sex and their connection with early sexual experiences.
- Define medical and anatomical limitations or options in developing a pleasurable sexual relationship.
- Acknowledge the differences between male and female sexual needs and motivations, and coordinate and adapt those with your own efforts, or seek professional help.
- Overcome some dysfunctional habits and adjust your partner's sexual habits that complicate sexual satisfaction for both partners.
- Constantly improve and renew sexual behavior and relations between you and your partner to develop harmony in your sexual relationship.
- Accept errors and shortcomings as the natural motion of human sexual relations.
- Accept nonconformities and limitations as natural physiological and psychological disharmony.
- Attempt to resolve sexual trauma or abuse experiences from the past. (Be open with your partner about this, if possible.)
- Constantly reveal and increase your attention to positive sexual experiences, including positive body images for you and your partner.
- Reexamine religious training in your view of sex and the basis of healthy laws of nature and balance in correspondence with rules in your community. In your interpretations of basic human values, consider relativity of at least 60 percent.
- Use healthy and sufficiently accurate knowledge of sexuality by freely acknowledging with your partner adequate

information about sexual functioning without reducing sex to the mechanical satisfaction of a vitally necessary function. Leave sufficient place for romanticism and the expression of feelings of love. Avoid jamming in the sexual freedom of the main system of values.

- It is necessary to be commensurate with your own sexual desires and the sexual desires of your partner. Be reasonable and unselfish.

- Share with your partner your own sexual desires using tactful, accurate, and descriptive language, including elements of sexual games and imagination in the healthy sense of their value.

- Settle conflicts that reflect sexual disharmony by realizing new options, desires, and needs. Also use appropriate coping strategies that reduce the negative impact of unsatisfied sexual interest or performance.

- Replace negative ways of thinking with positive ways that correspond to realistic interpretations and improve mood and sexual functioning.

- Remember that sexual attraction is connected with the reproductive function, a desire to have a reliable existence and secure life, health, sexual preferences, and religious beliefs, which complicate and limit the sexual lives of humans.

- Understand that sexual involvement in secret affairs might complicate and affect desirable sexual relationships.

ANGER

Anger is one of the unpleasant feelings we sometimes experience in extreme situations. Controlling anger and repressing its manifestation is necessary in order to establish a healthy expression of negative feelings and comfortably communicate with people. Some people show signs of anger at the slightest trigger and under any circumstances; regulating and controlling anger for such people is a stumbling block. Anger management is essential for them. An angry person is inclined to many forms of negative thinking: egocentric thinking, double standards, personalization, mental filters, catastrophization, all-or-nothing, white-and-black, predicting the future, emotional reasoning, blaming, fear of rejection or abandonment, projection, expecting punishment, thinking of revenge, jumping to conclusions, humiliation, using ultimatum words, etc.

Acting out, scandals, inability to establish smooth and good relations with others, constant disputes, and disputes without reasons, especially when the person feels a great injustice, are the main signs of anger. We can repeat here the fact that our feelings are concordant to our thinking, which is associated with basic values and supportive beliefs. For the most part, in therapy a psychologist tries to challenge or refine the interpretations of associated supportive beliefs, which are still connected by invisible threads to basic human values. Since a person learned negative ways of thinking and beliefs, it is possible for him or her to understand the problem and solve the cause of his or her irrational anger.

From this point of view, it is possible to conduct positive adjustment in thinking, which for some reason affects the behavior of irrational anger, and review the schemas that secure the boundaries of right and wrong thinking and behavior. A person's anger might be directed at other people and him—or herself; that determines the approach to this problem. Using positive interpretations of the actions and motives of other people based on real, relevant facts and data, and taking into account the total disharmony in the world will help identify the key to this problem.

Alternative solutions to anger

- Identify underlying beliefs that cause angry feelings and support irrational thoughts. Replace them with more functional, neutralizing anger and logical thinking in order to challenge them.
- Develop controlled expression of anger and treat others the way you wish to be treated.
- Accept the validity of disharmony and imperfections in the world that produce injustice and violations of the existing order. Learn to forgive and forget.
- Identify the negative impact of irrational, angry feelings and angry outbursts.
- Learn to express your anger in socially acceptable but not self-defeating ways in order to handle angry feelings without repressing the natural healthy reaction to the stimulus that caused the anger.

- Focus on positive developments and positive reality more than on the subject of your anger to work on the resolution of the problem instead reacting angrily. Again, break big problems into small steps and gradually reduce the imbalance and disharmony of the present situation, taking advantage of positive imagination and optimistic mood.
- Identify a model of appropriate anger expression; give yourself and others second, third, and more chances; and practice as often as possible using role-playing and modeling techniques.
- Come to terms with the fact that sometimes we cannot overcome difficulties without doubting our own abilities in different situations. Sometimes you can fail, and this is part of living life. Nobody is perfect.
- Learn your own body language to reduce tension and irritability. Control your facial expression, gestures, voice modulation, and phrases, as well as your behavior in terms of expressing your anger in calm and relaxed ways that are appropriate to the situation. Use muscle relaxation exercises.
- Accommodate other people's imperfections as well your own to develop patience.

MEMORY AND CONCENTRATION PROBLEMS

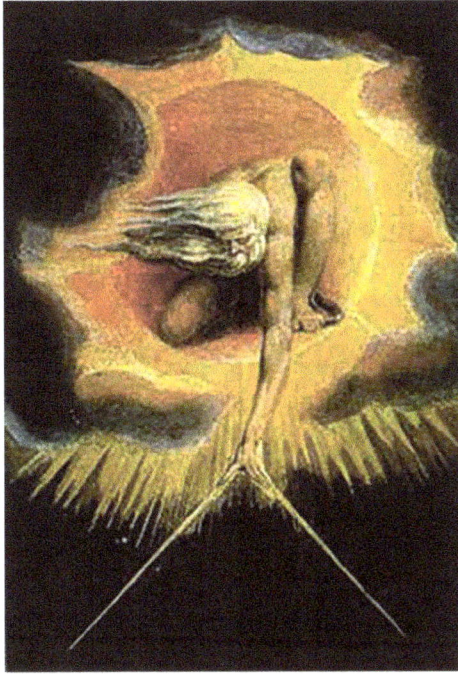

Memory is the amazing human ability to accumulate knowledge and experience, and it defines our success in many areas of life. Therefore, it is a very important function of daily creative activity in all fields and spheres of human cognition. Some mental disorders and medical conditions can interfere with this, increasingly eroding the exclusive ability of our brains to memorize and learn new information and store it. Some sources of information state that this great ability to memorize somehow depends on age, not biological differences, and more psychological approaches. These sources have stated that our way of memorizing depends on our specific method for categorizing, using positive imagery, or comparing.

These same sources cite children's extraordinary ability to memorize and learn absolutely new information by using positive imagery and comparison with bright identical images. They also point to examples of adults who show poor ability to reproduce an accurate picture of the images because they use categories (e.g., clothing, food, building materials, color, etc.) that obscure the specific and precise information in their memories and instead play familiar material.

Also known is the dependence of our ability to memorize on certain levels of neurohormones and the adequate supply of blood, oxygen, and nutrients to the brain. It is equally important to improve brain function with constant and adequate mental exercises, which can provide a high level of memorization, analysis, consolidation, and information storage. It is evident that constant mental exercise using brain cells might support appropriate memory and concentration with extensive use of stored information in humans. It has also been proven that depression, which is responsible for reducing some neurohormones, also significantly affects memory and concentration. All of this can explain impaired memory, which is produced when the depression drawback of serotonin, norepinephrine, and epinephrine affects the normal function of the brain and the use of our memory.

An overload of inaccurate, contradictory, and unrealistic information also disrupts normal use of memory. Memorized pieces of information that were already revised in the past can seriously impair memory and learning new data. The dysfunction of memory and concentration has led to distraction in many tasks and different information that is contradictive, uncertain, and nearly realistic. This includes the confidence that new information is incorrect or dubious because it does not meet the usual logic of such a person, who has a certain amount of information according to his or her belief system that excludes the other interpretation. Certain natural remedies that improve blood supply (*Ginkgo biloba*) and many others that increase certain neurohormones in the brain could be beneficial in some instances of memory and concentration disturbances. In severe cases and related medical conditions of memory loss, it is essential to take medications as prescribed by a doctor.

Alternative solutions for memory and concentration problems

- Identify sources and causes of reduction or loss in memory; come to terms with certain restrictions.
- Develop adaptive mechanisms such as making schedules; taking notes; writing lists of items you need to remember; marking your calendar entries in a diary; placing items in an easily detectable or very prominent place; repeating names, dates, and numbers two, three, or four times after hearing them the first time; comparing words, names, and data with familiar information or associating them with something familiar and similar; making funny drawings of things you need to buy at the grocery store or necessary daily responsibilities; and imagining how and when you need to do certain tasks and motivating yourself by imagining positive results in them.
- Establish routine tasks that involve repetition, and install a series of actions and activities daily or in a certain sequence to establish the order and automatism required to compensate for memory disturbances.
- Constantly add new elements in your daily activities, and plan a daily opportunity for enjoyment and entertainment to increase energy and motivation.
- Plan the enjoyable activities with routine, boring tasks at the same time.
- Concentrate on preferences rather than pleasure in performing daily tasks.
- Start your most enjoyable or preferable task first.
- Give yourself a break and rest. Plan enjoyable activities every day; you must provide respite and pause to switch focus and improve your functioning.
- Identify which activities are not improving your functional status and are associated with poorly controlled impulses or nonfunctional activities and hobbies that differ from useful, truly pleasurable activities.

ATTENTION DEFICIT HYPERACTIVE DISORDER

This condition typically affects children but can affect adults as well. Adults and children can share problems with education, impulsivity, irritability, overexcitability, outbursts of anger, and lack of concentration. Concentration problems also include evidence of distractibility and violation of attention by anything, distraction from principal ideas, and the inability to concentrate on a single thing for long periods of time. It can also be manifested in restlessness, fidgeting, and impulsivity that leads to impulsive decisions with harmful consequences for themselves and other people. The inability to maintain mood and mood swings often result in small frustrations that turn to anger or depression. It also prevents the establishment of proper mood; instead moods dip or spike, which makes it hard to arrange their lives and activities. Resolving conflicts with other people or children is also difficult.

This leads to deficiency in organizing all areas of life, which often affects patients who have difficulty finishing tasks and who are unable to clarify the goals and directions for those activities. For such conditions, low frustration and stress tolerance are key. They are what reflects poor control of thinking, feelings, and behavior. As a result, those symptoms support low self-esteem and addictive behavior.

It is essential for this condition to use strategies to develop coping mechanisms for attention and concentration problems. As discussed earlier, this includes identifying and establishing thinking and behavior that will help establish control and management of the symptoms. Amendment of nonfunctional thoughts and actions as well as correction of the belief and values system installations are crucial. Regulation and correction in thinking and behavior implies slow, step-by-step modifications with or without the help of a psychologist (psychotherapist) and sometimes with the support of medical treatment by a doctor. Self-encouragement and self-gratification for any small success are a necessary component in resolving these problems.

Alternative solutions for attention deficit hyperactive disorder

- Identify the symptoms and signs of the pathological condition and how they affect normal life and behavior.
- Install main and supportive goals in order to establish a graded transition to normal thinking and behavior. Resolving problems step-by-step will slowly reduce the negative effects of those symptoms on your life.
- Developing self-control strategies such as "stop, listen, think, and then act" can help curb impulsive behavior and strengthen your positive image of yourself.
- Engage in activities that do not include obsession with destroying your health such as eating your favorite food, listening to music, playing videogames for a specific amount of time each day, etc. Be sure to choose activities that reflect time limits to avoid the impulse of indulgence.

- Learn time-out intervention, a process in which you remove or distract yourself from provoking situations and find exits without undue excitement and action by switching to neutral and soothing options of normal and healthy reactions. As part of this, list what to expect from other people and improve communication skills.
- Use a calm, tranquil atmosphere and environment combined with distractions from annoying objects to develop relaxation skills and divert your attention toward other relaxing things; utilize a conflict-alarm system to lower threshold exposure to irritants.
- Reward each successful attempt in these complex adaptive activities and strategies by developing a self-rewarding system.
- Set a strict schedule of major and important activities using a graph sheet and sticky notes pasted in prominent places to maintain daily routines and better organization of your time and efforts.

CUTTING CLASSES

Unexplained absences from school are a burden for parents when suddenly they hear a message from the school about their children or teenagers. This usually results in a confrontation between the parents and the lazy pupils that affects the functioning of the whole family and produces a struggle between the two sides for what is right. If gaps in school attendance occur (this happens mostly in high school), it likely means that your child or teenager is experiencing all sorts of problems with school lessons, or that other teens have a bad influence on the academic achievement and the psyche of the teen, who can't cope with peer pressure or who acts under the influence of somebody in or outside of school. Oftentimes cutting classes means the protest of a child or teenager against neglect or a poor understanding or his or her needs and interests in the earlier child-parent relationship (even if these interests sometimes reflect awkward infatuations and overgeneralizations), and sometimes it is so far gone that it is difficult to stop or impede the harmful academic effects on the unlucky student.

The more recrimination and punishment parents and teachers give, the more resistance and stalling there will be from the child or adolescent in school. Parents' inability to establish appropriate control can sometimes allow the child to be successful in cutting classes. The neglect of old problems between the parents and the child or young person promotes the undesirable cutting of school.

However, numerous reports and memorandums, telephone calls, and face-to-face complaints from teachers to parents about poor grades and dips in test and examination scores, as well as expelling the student from school, can bring a stop to the precarious and frivolous behavior and help the student understand the seriousness of the situation. In this case, changing schools can make a difference, as can helping the child with homework, hiring a tutor, improving family relationships, giving the child enough meaningful time together with the whole family, practicing patience and love, and giving rewards for minor successes and efforts rather than giving presents or having boring conversations about how wrong the child's actions are as a precept or punishment.

On the other hand, it is important to remove all reasons that produce this behavior, establish understanding, and discourage outside communications with bad influences on the teen or child. Parents need to encourage only appropriate behavior and not press too hard for the child to accomplish the parents' goal to stop cutting classes. Also, in contrast to the tedious talk of obedience and commitment, it may be useful to express some solidarity in memories of the parents' own misconceptions and mistakes in childhood or adolescence. Pressing and serious punishment can harden and deepen controversy that is certainly linked with severe psychological problems and needs professional help.

Alternative solutions for cutting classes

- Identify the student's reasons for cutting class.
- Establish closer contact with each other and appropriate communications in the family.
- Restrict and discourage environments that are inappropriate for establishing normal behavior.
- Get acquainted with the peers of your child and define their bad influences on him or her (i.e., the reason for skipping lessons).
- Show understanding and sympathy for a child and his or her interests and predilections, and explain calmly and gracefully any detrimental impact on his or her fate and why some inventions and dreams may not be in the foreground.
- Give the child examples from the lives of other children and adults who could be positive role models for others to follow.
- Use the means of art and literature for more interesting and accessible communication with your child and as a way of better understanding their goals.
- Know how to impress your child without a great cost of money on games, clothing, and entertainment. Focus with all your attention and care on the child's ability to take pleasure from simple things that are interesting for him or her, and be willing to understand and help your child.
- Give the child some space or the silent treatment instead of arguments and conflicts.
- Make correct observations and discouragements by not satisfying the less important interests and pleasures of the child.
- Spend more time having fun together with the whole family in activities that have already proved themselves or that are new and interesting for everyone in the family.

Financial Problems

Financial problems are relevant and significant in the most modern and competitive countries, which require survival rules according to the fast-changing environments and rapid growth of knowledge, technology, and professional and educational criteria. Financial problems are not pleasant and often support depression, anxiety, and other psychological problems.

Financial problems are related to the ability of a person or group of people to make the right conclusions, embrace all circumstances in the financial world, and make fair choices. It relates to the impossibility of finding a job or the loss of employment; the lack of a livelihood to meet growing needs; credit card debt, loans for education, home mortgages; all sorts of unexpected fines, including health care and taxes; as well as increasing market prices. It covers a wide range of issues in the financial world and produces psychological and mental problems. Maniac depressive disorder, compulsive disorders, depression, general anxiety disorder, etc., might contribute to financial difficulties or be promoted as a result of financial difficulties because all of those mental conditions include disorders in thinking and behavior based on irrational beliefs that produce and support financial problems.

Most often the problem is excessive spending, unreasonable acquisition of things people don't need, or the interpretations of advertisements and sales efforts as the person's need for certain products. It also includes poor judgment in making decisions about whether or not to acquire things. A compulsion to buy also leads to serious financial problems or the inability to make decisions regarding the priority in buying things. In addition, the financial problems of patients as individuals with mental and other diseases may be associated with the cost of restoring their health: medications, payment for medical and hospital care; the inability to make money because of their disability or temporary disability.

It is difficult to predict how people with huge financial capabilities or spheres of influence in the financial world undergo mental disorders (temporary or permanent) and how this affects the economic balance and the rise of universal benefits. It is obvious that the stock transactions on Wall Street dependent on whether the investors believe in the success of financial contributions and the abilities of financial clerks to operate with their money. All financial companies and their products are based on the belief of others in the accuracy of information and belief in them, which contributes to the implementation of production. Dynamics and success of the material world in the developed economy depend on the reasonable and clear decisions of people who are making choices in financial operations and purchases of advertised products.

The variety of options, possibilities, and opportunities in developing new products define new and more advanced technologies and economic power, but they also give rise to financial problems that cause psychological problems and stress in different groups of people. Refusing to spend money or buy things might bring disarrangement to the development of the economic world and produce severe unpredictable financial problems. The economic world depends on the willingness and ability of people to put their money into developing the economy and their purchasing ability. Chaotically developing financial operations leads to limitations and obscure problems that are connected with crises in the financial world and the inability to predict the financial future of a large number of people.

If financial problems are not related to an economic crisis, then we can talk about mental conditions that give rise to them. Although the economic crisis may create temporary mental problems, they tend to go away after restoring economic well-being. It seems like this excludes the role of the basic belief system in the financial world, but in real-life situations it is very credible how people implement their own belief systems with the belief systems of others. If we need to discuss financial problems related to mental condition, then this is completely different. However, implications of motives for financial problems also might be based on interpretations of basic and supportive human beliefs.

Disharmony in the belief system that results in disharmony in mental conditions of humans reflects disharmony in the economic and financial development of society. It is seemingly a value system, and its applications to financial problems are far from each other, but in fact there is a close and substantial connection between the two (i.e., how people apply moral rules and the basic value system in accordance with financial operations by supporting their financial existence). As such, interpretations and basic offers that are related to human values are based on the direct route to success in the financial well-being of individuals and society as a whole.

Disharmony in the system's core values, as well as mental disorders, can seriously disrupt the economic world and the implications of it, and contribute to or exacerbate financial problems and the emergence of mental conditions relating to them. If a person's financial problems are not dependent on the economic crisis, he or she should be trained to control his or her financial affairs. This should be done using the appropriate strategy and the formulation of an adaptive mechanism. The first thing to establish is the availability of affordable income or income sources. Then one must control the misuse of funds and financial operations, including meeting basic needs and their limited capacity.

Then establishment of control over spending is necessary, including all needs and limitations at the present time. This control includes reestablishing beliefs that produce negative ways thinking that support financial problems. These include perfectionism, dependency, low self-esteem, humiliation, projection, hopelessness, magnification or minimization, personalization, mixing thought with fact, double standards, egocentrism, tunnel vision, mental filters, etc. In most instances the person needs to build self-respect, have limited financial means, stop exaggerating the power of money, increase feelings of self-worth and self-confidence, look to the security of promoting his or her own health and spiritual interests, and save for future financial possibilities and financial success by focusing on activities unrelated to the spending of money. All of this will reinforce the person's belief that the value of a human being is bigger than the value of material goods, as well as restore his or her faith in morals and other valuable things in the world.

Mental health problems may also raise a conflict between internal moral requirements and the level of financial need. Constant thoughts about the unfairness of financial regulation may also contribute to depression, anxiety, panic attacks, and other mental disorders. At the same time, refusing to increase financial stability and corresponding earnings could also lead to instability and vulnerability of mental health and human well-being. Striking a balance between needs and efforts to alleviate financial struggles in accordance with the rules and laws of society may build self-motivation and a healthy interest in life and in meeting a person's financial and psychological needs.

Alternative solutions for financial problems

- Establish the fact of and reasons for the financial difficulties by accurately identifying the financial obligations and problems on the worksheet.
- Identify the dysfunctional beliefs and supportive types of negative thinking that are contributing to your financial problems.

- Consider and develop a more appropriate strategy to eliminate the financial problems.
- Reduce feelings of hopelessness and any ideas of suicide when choosing the path out of a financial predicament. Go through all the available options for tasks and ideas to establish suicide-free choices.
- Immediately seek the help of agencies for social and financial assistance, as well as individuals who can provide financial advice; file for bankruptcy using the services of a lawyer; get a loan with a low-interest credit card or a debt obligation with a small monthly price; or ask for help from family members or friends.
- Identify your main mistake and build a strategy for financial independence.
- Develop spending priorities.
- Develop the ability to install a cost-efficient way of payment.
- Identify options for immediate financial relief.
- Develop a financial plan and overlook budget.
- Recognize your own emotional vulnerability in spending and your mood swings.
- Plan a job search to gain appropriate income.
- Make financial records every day.
- Gain control of your urge to spend money.
- Learn purchase delay.
- Use an appropriate role-model in gaining financial control.
- Develop resistance to external pressure to spend money beyond what you can afford.
- Develop the ability to make appropriate decisions by estimating pros and cons.
- Concentrate on your efforts to resolve your debts, and gain pride and self-confidence.

PARENTING PROBLEMS

Parenting problems reflect many difficulties in the absence of experience and the effects of pressure in the unfavorable environments in which parents raise children—misbehavior, refusing to get homework right, screaming, breaking things, being late, not listening to requests and remarks, you can name it. But these are not the most difficult challenges that lie ahead in the later period of rearing grown children. Children's trust can be undivided in their first five years or so; however, their search for their own integrity, answers, and experiences soon becomes discordant to the parents' thoughts about how things need to be.

Gaining the respect and trust of a child is a difficult task that depends not only on the personalities and skills of the parents but also on the nature and inclinations of the child at any age (taking into account the role of mental deviations from the so-called norms.) We can be more thoughtful if we recall our own childhoods. Then things can be more easily understood. Along with rigorous approaches to children's and adolescents' norms of behavior, individual biases and deviations that are appropriate in modern society and contribute to the development of harmonious and even extraordinary personalities in society have appeared.

Standard views of how it should and should not be hinder the development of individuality in a child and impede the progressive growth of society. Often this understanding is limited only by inconsistency with parents in the past and does not exclude errors and misconceptions in other areas of education or the need for advice and support from a psychologist or a professional specialist. Often the untruthfulness and rationality of parents prevent the child from getting to the truth and making his or her own correct assessments and decisions in the future.

Explanations of the benefits and necessary contrary wishes and whims of the child do not increase rapport with parents. The forms in which adults put their ideas, even correct ones, need the use of illustrative fantasies and imagination, which adults forget to enjoy under the heavy burden of daily tasks, which are actually rejected by children. Parents unconsciously provide inaccurate or inappropriate information about the future, which promotes distrust and disagreements when kids grow up. We give untruthful information to children: we teach them things we do not truly believe just to get things straight at the present moment, and we don't give thought to how those lies will affect our future relationships with and the trust of our children.

Parental care is often hard when it comes to things and wealth (without explanations of spiritual values or things that provide pleasure) that do not cost money. We concentrate on giving things and meeting children's needs without teaching basic values based on our own examples. As a result, we set double standards for our children: We can do things that they are not allowed to do. We cannot accept that children do not achieve the desired perfection, but we tolerate it when we do not achieve it. We are afraid to admit to our children that we are not perfect, and this is fine. This is in human nature. We support perfectionism in our children, which ultimately promotes disappointment, low self-esteem, dependency, and the inability to function normally in society.

We forget to teach children gratitude toward others, including us (their parents), which leads to their indifference and ingratitude toward us when they grow up. We hope the difficulties of life will teach them on their own without our efforts, and as a result we grow future "monsters" who hate their parents and hold a legitimate place for this hate. We miss the chance when our children believe and depend on us to develop in them the ability to coordinate their personal interests with those of others, including parents, in any period of their lives. We are forgetting to teach our children to not be just takers but instead to be givers, and we give them little education about how to share good and bad things with all members of the family.

Expectations of appreciation from children and the desire to be surrounded by caring human support in old age and illnesses, as usually happens in friendly relations between people, sometimes suffer disappointment and collapse. This may be the most controversial area of outstanding issues in human relations. Religion is simple and clear: everybody takes care of their parents. Society also takes both tasks on, which sometimes stimulates the loss of custody of children and provides social services for older people. In some cases, spiritual connections can be stronger than financial relations between generations—parents and children.

There is also a strong relationship when the material interests of the subject of negotiation are spiritual. Parents retain their unique right to put their dreams and possibilities into their children, despite the intervention of societal standards and regulations in these natural tendencies. Although in both cases there are extremes in presenting reasonable boundaries.

A simple task of every parent is to let his or her child be successful in completing the duties set by society in order to show the child his or her greatest ability in determining social status and achieve self-sufficiency. In contrast to spoiled children, those who grew in balanced environments with respect for their parents learn quickly to satisfy their own interests while at the same time not forgetting their duty toward their parents.

Those children better comply with the requirements of society. Some parents are trying to delay children's transition to self-sufficiency and are therefore disturbing the balance in the interests of the child, society, sometimes them (the parents). However, in some instances the children gain unreasonable guilt, and in order to repay this unreasonable guilt, they sacrifice their essential needs and fail to accomplish the main goals of their lives. We don't make a purpose of holding our children in constant guilt and feelings of the need to repay all the things we did for them; we just have hope that they will be grateful and make some effort to help their parents in the future. We need to pay attention to who we are and who our children will become in our intentions to give them love and everything they or we desire.

Parents' dreams can be realized in their children. A variety of personalities and different kinds of destiny depend on the realization of those dreams. A simple task for any parent is to help his or her child be successful and gain an independent way of life (using appropriate parental help). The best means for the success of your child is to teach the child to get things on his or her own rather than making everything easy and available at any time, which only supports dependency and the child's feeling that he or she is unable to meet his or her own needs without your help. Giving guidance, support, and reasonable help are very functional instruments in your parental mission. Encouragement and discouragement are parental tools in raising mentally healthy children without forceful intervention.

Parental tools do not include psychological and physical abuse and punishment, or the imposition of unrealistic goals for the child's age. Neither do parental duties include the physical, verbal, or sexual abuse that we have witnessed in some instances. Abused children also learn that this is the only right way to raise children, which will affect their parenting in the future. Children who were abused in childhood might be mentally ill and can't accomplish any simple goal that they might have reached in a healthy family.

All of these parental aspirations will serve as examples for a harmonious future of new families. In the case of child abuse, they will complicate the challenges the future generation has in raising their own children. Of course, common strategies are inadequate for children in cases of mental health problems and require constant assistance of parents by social services to improve the child's achievement and progress, as well as achieve the recovery of the child.

Alternative solutions for parenting problems

- Constantly together with your child, learn to build a functional system of values and ways to fulfill the child's needs without undermining his or her foundations.
- Learn to modify your dysfunctional beliefs, thinking, and behavior—for example, feeding a bad example to the child—and teach him or her the same thing.
- Accustom a child to controlling his or her moods through positive repetition of utterances that express negative thinking; this will help him or her cope with unpleasant feelings and learn how to be adaptive to environmental changes without stress.
- Teach the child to face fear by gradually overcoming his or her status (experiencing frustration and disappointment) and removing triggers. This can be accomplished under the control of a parent or other older individual by overcoming difficulties in certain situations (activities including fear of going to school, talking and socializing with other children, and so on) step-by-step.
- Reduce your own dysfunctional response to the child's behavior by controlling your thoughts and clarifying your beliefs that contribute to excessive anxiety.
- Bring up your own responsibilities together with demands of the same from the child.
- Use role-playing and modeling techniques (e.g., child imagination, games, and made-up expressions of history) to develop adequate conduct of the child.

- Use positive examples and images of role models, including yourself.
- Ignore and extinguish dysfunctional behaviors and speech of the child.
- Respond in an empathic way to the child's worries or concerns, without reinforcing or simply dismissing them.
- Spend enough time in group activities with the child to develop trust, respect, and positive emotional dialogue with each other.
- Be reasonable your requirements of the child with respect to his or her achievements and failures, interests and needs.
- Bear in mind the influence of peer pressure that interferes with the child's success in improving his or her dysfunctional behavior and cognitions.
- Consult with a psychologist or a professional in various education and child behavior problems; use coaching and counseling in difficulties with your child's behavior and negative thinking before they become a problem.
- Treat the child for serious medical and mental disorders by using medications if he or she needs them.
- Continuously monitor your own dysfunctional negative beliefs, thoughts, feelings, and behavior.

Educational Problems of Children

Children's education is based on learning at school and at home as a result of common efforts to empower them with knowledge so that they may successfully complete their main tasks in the future. A child's ability to grasp information in fast, amazing ways or completely ignore studying necessary items for his or her education may please or upset parents and schoolteachers.

When children show interest in knowledge, books, and educational games and entertainment, parents can encourage them in such trends by displaying adequate interest and support. Parents can help their children achieve success in school by explaining the value and importance certain knowledge and subjects will have later in life and by providing real examples of knowledge that improved or changed their own lives as a result of intensive and productive studying. Then the child might show progress and success in his or her school.

Additional methods for significant impact on promoting good school performance for kids can be asking how school went without expressing severely affective remarks at the wrong actions of the child. Instead, parents need to show understanding and appropriate responses. For example, the parent could say how he or she would have behaved in this life situation in matters of daily events at school or show compassion and give examples from his or her past school life without excessive criticism and lecturing. Parents should ask about the child's difficulties in school at least every two to three days if the child is experiencing problems. In some cases, it will be reasonable and efficient to hire a tutor.

Parents need to organize the child's daily tasks and a location for studying. Before parents help with homework, it might be appropriate to give the child one more chance to do the task on his or her own. It is powerful—despite the large role of the Internet, television and other media opportunities—if the child is interested in reading, which develops spelling and language skills, increases information gained, and improves speech and communication with others. Parents would do well to get a list of books for children from their child's classroom teacher and read them together with the child.

Television, movies, video games, museums, exhibitions, and other events can be educational, but only in reasonable quantities that also include physical education and strengthening of healthy activities and other recreations for the child. Games that do not require large financial expense but engage the imagination of the child with the characters and the games they play, as well as stories from books, movies, and video games, will motivate the child's actions, desires, and challenges. Gathering and playing with other kids is also very educational and contributes to the child's different motivations in studying, gaining other kinds of information and skills that are exciting, and developing imagination and the ability to model different life situations that are essential in social life. However, instead of being favorable, the influence might be the very opposite, which is why flexible and sensitive control of the adverse influence of peers by parents is crucial in preventing the development of learning problems at school.

Parents need to encourage the use of sources of accurate information, such as handbooks, dictionaries, and reference books, in addition to other exciting and colorful sources that include children's games, video games, movies, the Internet, and television. Some psychologists believe that education should be emphasized under the ages of fourteen to seventeen years old because puberty diverts teens from the educational course, diminishing the intensity of their training. In other instances, some teenagers become more motivated and display more effort and interest in studying. Frequent encouragement and praise is more effective with children of this age than boring edification. Every student needs understanding and assistance in overcoming difficulties in learning advanced knowledge. The most vivid talents and abilities manifest at this age and, increasingly, are giving good results in the future, although there is no absolute proof.

Development of thinking abilities, the ability to apply knowledge, and the ability to contribute to a large extent increases children's progress toward further success, while promoting recognition and identification of the virtues of parents and society will not. Children with mental and psychological problems, especially retardation, need encouragement and recognition for their zeal in training, which can bring about satisfactory results. You must clearly understand the limitations and difficulties of such children without overtaxing their efforts; otherwise, it can lead to great disappointments for both parties. These assessments are determined by the appropriate level of development and constant encouragement of such children. Some parents can't accept the mental and psychological limitations of their children and contribute to negative ways of thinking (e.g., perfectionism and exaggeration of understating), which amplifies the frustration and future mental health problems of these children.

Children who exhibit extraordinary abilities and talents in early development might fail for many reasons (fatigue, stress, and adversity in life) that result from extreme tiredness and the inability to handle life stressors. In addition, some children who do not show a notable success at an early age can make a significant advance in later stages of their development, although this is less likely.

Some children who are very promising in the beginning of their schooling might fail in the future, while other children who do not show special results early on might be successful and very productive in other periods of their life spans. In cases when parents do not recognize their high achievement standards for younger children, they need to realize that there is no reason to push a child to study and put huge efforts into areas of knowledge that are not in their power to overcome or embrace.

However, along with this, children who try to work hard more effectively achieve success without harm to their health, particularly their mental health, and gradually expand that success. Anybody who tries hard enough might get something lesser but still prominent and remarkable as a result of those efforts. Intellectual development in mentally and physically healthy individuals who can apply their knowledge in life and work is the goal of modern education.

Alternative solutions to children's educational problems:

- Determine the strengths and weaknesses of your child's efforts in learning at school.
- Install and support the special interests of the child.
- Arrange the child's daily activities and a good, well-organized location for studying.
- Teach the child to attach importance to accurate facts from reliable sources of information.
- Forgive the child, and don't just focus on errors in his or her efforts to learn, especially if he or she recognizes them.
- Use the cognitive rehearsal technique for reducing mistakes and disappointments. Identify the type of negative thinking and behaviors in the child (e.g., perfectionism, double standards, mistaken identity, magnification or minimization, egocentrism, projection of thoughts onto other people, self-criticism, shyness, shame, tunnel vision, etc.) and use modification of attitudes and behavior to reduce the child's errors and disappointments.

- Use imagery in studying and organizing places for the improvement of learning.
- Accustom a child to everyday homework and tasks, which causes him or her to gradually accumulate knowledge and pacing; systematize the acquisition of information; and concentrate on his or her efforts in learning.
- Motivate and promote yourself and the child, improve outcomes of studying, recognize any achievements in his or her learning, and reward him or her for each accomplishment.
- Read more books, which is the equivalent to a nice conversation with a smart person, and discuss topics with people who can replace reading the smartest book.
- Plan each day to gain new steps and opportunities in increasing educational progress and knowledge.
- At first your child should spend more time with easier and more interesting subjects, although the order may be changed according to need.
- Give your child a rest and a chance to have fun in short intermediate periods between studying.
- Teach a child not to be shy and to ask questions of his or her teacher, classmates, parents, friends, and others.
- Train a child to correctly and competently express him—or herself, watch his or her speech as it develops, and take advantage of proven facts and data.
- Remember that any small result is better than nothing, and trying is worth more than doing nothing.

REFERENCES

Мечников И.И. Этюды о природе человека. (1905) Второе издание.

Чуковкий К.И. О Чехове: Человек и мастер.—3-е изд. 2007. 208 с., ил. ISBN 978-5-85887-263-4.

Пять книг торы.(Текст сверен с рукописью и масорой Кэтэр Арам Цовы и сходных с ней рукописей Мордыхаем Броером), русский перевод Давида йосифона, Хемед, йерушалаим 5738 (1978).

Елена Левенталь. Характеры и роли - М.: Триада, 2006. - 320с. ISBN 5-86181-350-7

Дейл Карнеги. Как завоёвывать друзей. Минск, 2004, ISBN 985-14-0817-4.

Beck, Aaron T. 1990. *Cognitive Therapy of Personality Disorders.* New York: The Guilford Press.

Beck, Aaron T., A. John Rush, Brian F. Shaw, and Gary Emery. 1979. *Cognitive Therapy of Depression.* USA:.

Beck, Judith S. 1995. *Cognitive Therapy. Basics and Beyond.* New York: The Guilford Press.

Corey, Gerald. 1977. *Theory and Practice of Counseling and Psychotherapy.* 5th ed. California:. Glibert, Paul. 1999. *Overcoming Depression.* New York:.

Hawton, Keith, Paul M. Salkovskis, Joan Kirk, and David M. Clark. 1998. *Cognitive Behavior Therapy for Psychiatric Problems A Practical Guide.* Great Britain:. First published 1989.

Jongsma Jr., Arthur E. and L. Mark Peterson. 1995. *The Complete Psychotherapy Treatment Planner.* USA:.

—. 2000. *The Severe and Persistent Mental Illness TreatmentPlanner.* USA:.

—. 2001. *The Adult Psychotherapy Progress Notes Planner.* New York:.

Kahn, Michael. 2002. *Basic Freud: Psychoanalytic Thought For the Twenty First Centuries.* USA:.

Kaplan, Harold I. and Benjamin J. Sadock. 1996. *Pocket Handbook of Clinical Psychiatry.* 2nd ed. USA:.

Kaplan, Stanley H. 1987. *Behavioral Science Notes.* USA: Educational Center.

Meissner, W.W. 2000. *Freud and Psychoanalysis.* Indiana:.

Persons, Jacqueline B. 1989. *Cognitive Therapy in Practice. A Case FormulationApproach.* New York:.

Phaidon. 1998. *The Art Book.* London:.

Rabberg, Celia. 2007. *Do You Get The Feeling?* Bloomington, IN: AuthorHouse.

Sadock, Benjamin J. and Virginia A. Sadock. 2003. *Kaplan & Sadock's Synopsis of Psychiatry: Behavioral Sciences/Clinical Psychiatry.* 9th ed. USA: Lippincott Williams & Wilkins.

Sallard, Paul. 2005. *A Clinician's Guide to Think Good—Feel Good. Using CBT with children and young people.* England:.

Wiener, Jerry M. and Nancy A. Breslin. 1995. *The Behavioral Sciences in Psychiatry.* 3rd ed.

LIST OF THE PAINTINGS

Маринус Ван Реймейрсвале 1493-1567, Сборщики податей
Marinus Van Roymerswaele (Roemerswaele) (Reymerswael). Percepteus
D'Impots. Hermitage Museum, Saint Petersburg, Russia

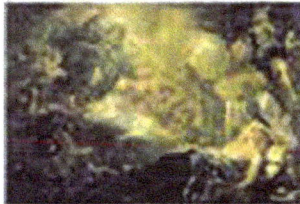

The Dream of Solomon. 1693. Luca Giordano. 1632-1705. Naples

The Sacrifice of Isaac. 1620. Domenichrno (Domenico Zampieri).
1581-1641. Bolognia.

Antoine Watteau, 1684-1721, La Boudeuse.
Антуан Ватто. Капризница. 1718. <u>Hermitage Museum</u>, Saint Petersburg,
Russia

Moses and Aaron before Pharaoh: An Allegory of the Dinteville Family,
1537 Master of the Dinteville Allegory (Netherlandish or French, active
mid-16th century), Wentworth Fund.

Esther before Ahasuerus
Artemisia Gentileschi (Italian, Roman, 1593-1651/53),
The Metropolitan Museum of Art.

The Stolen Kiss, 1756-61.
Jean Honore Fragonard (French, 1732-1806), Hermitage.

The Death of Socrates, 1787.
Jacques-Louis David (French, 1748-1825)
Oil on canvas; 51 x 77 1/4 in. (129.5 x 196.2 cm)
Catharine Lorillard Wolfe Collection, Wolfe Fund, 1931 (31.45)

The Last Supper. 1652. Philippe de Champaigne, 1602-1674. Museum de Louvre, Paris.

The Death of Major Pierson. 1782-4. John Singleton Copley, 1738-1815, Tale Gallery, London

Holiday (The Picnic). 1876. James Tissot.l836-1902I-O Tale Gallery, London.

The Marriage Feast at Cana.1511. Gerard David. 1450-1523, Museum de Louvre, Paris.

F.X.Leyendecker, The Flapper, 1922

Pierre-Auguste Renoir, Le Moulin de la Gallete, 1876

William Blake, Newton, 1975

Pal-Ket. 1908, Victor Vasarely, Museo de Bellas Artes, Bilbao.

Head+Light+Surroundings. Umberto Boccioni.1912. Paolo Baldacci Gallery, NY

Kazimir Malevich, Messerschiefer(Prinzip des Flimmerns), 1913

Pablo Picasso, Bathers, 1918

Геракл, 1611. Дубовая доска, масло, 220x220. Дрезденская Картинная Галерея, Германия

Mark Gerter(1891-1939) Merry-GO-Round,1916, Tate Gallery

Blond Man, Roger de la Fresnaye—1922

John Everett Millais (1829-1896), Ophelia, 1851

Severin Kroyer Peter (1851—1909). Summer Evening on the Southern Beach. 1893. Skagens Museum

Carlo Carra (1866-1966). The Metaphysical Muse. 1917. Milan.

Caravaggio (1571-1610). Doubting Thomas. 1599. Potsdam.

Brown Ford Madox. Work. 1852-65. Manchester City Art Gallery.

Bathing of a Red Horse (Petrov-Vodkin), 1912

Vouet Simon. Time Overcome by Hope, Love and Beauty. 1627, Museum del Prado, Madrid.

Speeding Train by Ivo Pannaggi 1922

Seurat Georges. A Sunday Afternoon on the Island of La Grande Jatte. 1884-6, Chicago

Sanchez-Cotan Juan. Still Life, 1600-10, Private Collection.

Reni Guido. Saint Jerome and Angel, 1640-42, Detroit Institute of Art.

Tiziano Vecellio. Marie-Madeleine (La Madeleine) 1560
Тициан /Тициано Вечеллио/ 1485и1490-1576—Кающаяся Мария Магдалина. Гос. Эрмитаж.

Франциско де Сурбаран (около 1598-1664)
Испанская школа. Отрочество мадонны. Около 1660. Гос. Эрмитаж.
Francisco De Zurbaran
L'Adolescence De La Vierge Marie

И.Е.Репин. Иван Грозный и сын его Иван 16 ноября 1581года. Государственная Третьяковская галерея. Москва.
Ilya Repin. Tsar Ivan the Terrible and Is Son Ivan on November 16, 1581

В.В.Пукирев. Неравный брак. 1862. Государственная Третьяковская Галлерея
Vasily Pukirev. Mesalliance.

Otto Dix, The Nun, 1914

В.В. Верещагин. Апофеоз войны. 1971. Государственная Третьяковская Галлерея
Vasily Vereschagin. Apotheosis of War. 1871

Vasily Vereschagin. Near Moscow Waiting
for a Boyar Delegation. 1891-92. В.В.Верещагин. Перед Москвой в ожидании депутации бояр. 1891-92. Гос. Исторический музей.

Paul Klee, Analysis Verschiedener Perversitaten, 1922

Kazimir Malevich, Suprematism, 1915

Rembrandt Harmensz Van Rijn 1606-1669
Retour De L'Enfant Prodigue. 1668-1669
Рембрант Харменс Ван Рейн. Возвращение блудного сына. Гос. Эрмитаж.

Джорджоне Да Кастельфранко 1479/ 7/-1510 Юдифь. Гос. Эрмитаж.
Giorgione Da Castelfranco. Judith

Adrian Van Ostade.1610-1685. La Bagarre.
1637 Адриан Ван Остаде. Драка. Гос. Музей имени Пушкина.

On the way. Bad News from France.1887-95, Vasily Vereschagin.
На этапе. Дурные вести из Франции. 1887-95, В.В. Верещагин. Гос.
Исторический музей.

In Defeated Moscow ("Arsonists" or "Shooting in the Kremlin") 1897-98
Vasily Vereshagin.
В покорённой Москве ("Поджигатели" или "Расстрел в кремле")
Гос. Исторический музей

Scream.1893. Edvard Munch (1863-1944). National Gallery. Oslo.

Варварская Галлерея. Святой Себастьян.Тициан. 1956 (Тициано Вечеллио)
Tiziano Vecellio, 1490-1576. Saint Sebastian. Hermitage.

Friedrich Caspar David. The Wreck of the Hope, 1824, Hamburg

The Trial of Willam Lord Russel in 1683 by GH - Ferens Art Gallery

Jheronimus Bosch (1450-1516), Triptych of Earthly Delights

Pierre Puvis de Chavannes, Insane Woman in the Beach, 1887
In the Hermitage since 1931, Inv. No. 6564

Pierre-Auguste Renoir, On the Terrace, 1881

Бернардо Строцци. 1581-1644, Старая кокетка.
Гос. музей им. Пушкина
Bernardo Strozzi. Vanitas.

John William, (1861-1922) Youth and Time

Кузьма Петров-Водкин,1918 год в Петрограде (Петргоградская мадонна), 1920. Гос.Третьяковская галлерея. Моква.

Кузьма Петров-Водкин,1919—год. Тревога, 1934. Гос Русский музей. Ленинград.

Kazimir Malevich, Vanity Box, 1913

De Hooch. 1629-1884. Woman and a Maid with a Pail in a Courtyard. Hermitage.

Lippi Filippino. Portrait of an Old Man, 1457-1504, In Galleria degli Uffizi, Florence.

Lucas van Leyden, The Card Players, 1494-1533. Wilton House, Salisbury

Luke Filders "The Doctor"(1887)

Caillebotte Gustave. 1848-1894. Young Man at the Window. 1876. Paris.

William Blake, The Ancient of Days,

Fernand Leger. 1811-1955. Composition.

Gerard Van Honthorst (Gerardo Della Notte) 1590-1656. Saint Joseph
Le Charpantier. Герард ван Хонтхорст (Герардо Ночной) Детство
Христа. 1628. Hermitage.

Jacob Jordaens. 1593-1678. Le Roi Boit
Якоб Иорданс. Бобовый король. Louvre. Paris.

Henri Le Fauconnier. A Little School Girl. 1907. In the Hermitage.

http://commons.wikimedia.org/wiki/File:Briullov,_Karl_-_A_Dream_of_a_Girl_Before_a_Sunrise.jpg

http://en.m.wikipedia.org/wiki/File:Popova_Air_Man_Space.jpg

http://commons.wikimedia.org/wiki/File:Cezanne_Harlequin.JPG

http://en.wikipedia.org/wiki/Insane_Woman#mediaviewer/File:The_
mad_woman-Theodore_
Gericault-MBA_Lyon_B825-IMG_0477.jpg

www.ingramcontent.com/pod-product-compliance
Lightning Source LLC
Chambersburg PA
CBHW051243020426

42333CB00025B/3026